THE COLLABORATIVE CLASSROOM

50 Cooperative Learning Strategies for Student Engagement

BONEY NATHAN

Published in 2024 by Amba Press, Melbourne, Australia
www.ambapress.com.au

© Boney Nathan 2024

All rights reserved. No part of this book may be reproduced or transmitted in any form or by any means, electronic or mechanical, including photocopying, recording or by any information storage and retrieval system, without prior permission in writing from the publisher.

Originally published in 2021 by TellWell Talent.
This edition supersedes any previous edition.

Cover design: Luke Harris

ISBN: 9781923116191 (pbk)
ISBN: 9781923116733 (ebk)

A catalogue record for this book is available from the National Library of Australia.

To all teachers, we heard you.

"None of us is as smart as all of us"
-Sir Ken Robinson-

CONTENTS

	Introduction	1
	Cooperative Learning Elements	2
1.	Spider Web	7
2.	Exit Pass	9
3.	Find A Buddy Who	11
4.	Give 1 Get 1	13
5.	Hot Potato	15
6.	Inside Outside Circle	17
7.	K-W-L	19
8.	Think-Ink-Pair-Share	21
9.	Think-Pair-Share	23
10.	Turn and Talk	25
11.	Two-Minute Interview	27
12.	Word Wall	29
13.	ABC Summaries	31
14.	Chunking	33
15.	Dictionary Loop	35
16.	Placemat	37
17.	Round Robin	39
18.	Scavenger Hunt	41
19.	Talking Stick	45
20.	Team Pair Solo	47
21.	Three-Step Interview	49
22.	3-2-1 Strategy	51
23.	Agreement Circles	53
24.	Ask-n-Switch	55
25.	Concept Attainment	57

26.	Dialogue Map	59
27.	Fishbowl	61
28.	Fishbone	63
29.	Fix It	65
30.	Four Corners	67
31.	Frayer Model	69
32.	Graffiti Wall	71
33.	Literature Circles	73
34.	Loop It	77
35.	Numbered Heads Together	79
36.	PMI	81
37.	Quiz, Quiz, Trade	83
38.	Send a Problem	85
39.	Sticky Note Graph	87
40.	Y Chart	89
41.	Author's Gallery Walk	91
42.	Book Talk	95
43.	Case Studies	99
44.	Causal Mapping	101
45.	Cubing	103
46.	Inventors	105
47.	Jigsaws	109
48.	Mind Maps	111
49.	Three-Role Interview	113
50.	Write 'n' Pass	115

Introduction

There are ten elements highlighted in the research based High Impact Teaching Strategies:

- Setting Goals
- Structuring Lessons
- Explicit Teaching
- Worked Examples
- Collaborative Learning
- Multiple Exposures
- Questioning
- Feedback
- Metacognitive Strategies
- Differentiated Teaching

Cooperative Learning Strategies allow space for all these elements to occur implicitly and explicitly during teaching and learning practices.

Why this book?

- Teachers often approach us asking for explicit, step by step instructions to help them plan lessons that include the High Impact Teaching Strategies.
- There are many strategies online, but they are not easy to find unless you know the names and feel confident to adopt and adapt them to suit their contexts.
- We decided to investigate and collate fifty strategies in this book to help teachers have easy access and explicit instructions on how they can practically use them in their classrooms.
- We have also endeavoured to include as many online teaching ideas as possible to help teachers include some of these strategies during remote learning.

Why Cooperative Learning?

- These strategies can be used across the curriculum in various subject areas.
- They allow movement and differentiation to target individual student needs.
- They cover all four macro skills - listening, speaking, reading, and writing.
- They include various types of collaborative skills such as, pair work, group work, and allow students to gain confidence to continue working independently after the collaboration.
- They increase the level of engagement amongst students.
- They create a balance between safety and accountability.
- We are preparing students for jobs that may not exist yet. Cooperative learning strategies train students to have the emotional intelligence and social skills to function optimally in the real world when working in teams.
- They can be embedded in many parts of the Gradual Release Model.
- They allow teachers to monitor student progress.

How can you use them?

- We do not need to do cooperative learning strategies every day in every lesson.
- Practice makes Progress - We keep repeating one strategy until students and teachers are very familiar with it before moving on to a new strategy.
  e.g.: 1 strategy can be repeated over 5 weeks in different areas of a lesson.
- Conscious planning and preparation are the keys to successfully using and implementing cooperative learning strategies in our classrooms.

Cooperative Learning Elements

What is cooperative learning?

- Sparked by the research - Johnson, D., Maruyama, G., Johnson, R., Nelson, D., & Skon, L. (1981).
- A pedagogical process that allows active participation in the classroom.
- Active participation happens when more students are more engaged, more of the time.
- Promotes collaboration, social skills, and higher levels of student engagement.
- Small group of learners work together to achieve higher levels of success in tasks.
- Can be used for any year level and in any subject area.
- Develops metacognitive skills and covers multiple domains of Bloom's Taxonomy.
- Allows teachers to develop high impact teaching strategies.

What are the elements of Cooperative Learning?

- Face-to-Face Interaction / Promotive Interaction
- Safety and Individual Accountability
- Interpersonal and small group skills / Social Skills
- Positive Interdependence:
    - Goal Interdependence
    - Role Interdependence
    - Resource Interdependence
    - Incentive Interdependence
    - Outside Force Interdependence
    - Environmental Interdependence
    - Identity Interdependence
    - Sequence Interdependence
    - Simulation Interdependence
- Group Processing

Face-to-Face Interaction / Promotive Interaction

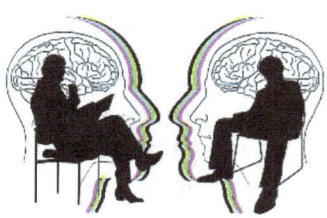

- Involves student engagement and interaction with one another.
- May happen when students are either working in pairs or groups.
- Allows maximum opportunities for encouragement, support, peer feedback, healthy debate or discussion, and praise.
- Indirectly increases the level of motivation amongst students.
- Happens when students:

    a. teach members of the group how to find solutions to problems.
    b. provide further explanation about a topic to the group members.
    c. discuss new ideas orally in pairs or groups.
    d. support one another in understanding the content of the lesson.

Safety and Individual Accountability

- Safety and accountability are like the two sides of a scale.
- If the task or activity is too safe, the advanced students may not participate. e.g.: A question or task that is not challenging and has obvious answers.
- If the task or activity is too accountable, the struggling students may not attempt it or just give up. e.g.: A task with unclear instructions, and too difficult to complete.
- For active participation to happen, there needs to be a balance between safety and accountability.

    e.g.: Teacher allows students to discuss a question with their partner for five seconds (**safety**) before calling their names by randomly picking pop sticks labelled with students' names (**accountability**).
- All cooperative learning strategies tick the safety and accountability boxes.

Interpersonal/Social Skills

- Involves teamwork skills, as part of a group.
- Allows maximum opportunities for encouragement, support, leadership, making decisions, healthy debate, or discussion, and managing conflict amongst group members.
- Indirectly increases the level of motivation.
- Happens when students:
    a. communicate in groups to come up with a decision or to find solution to a problem,
    b. praise or provide constructive criticism to group members
    c. discuss ideas in groups to complete tasks
    d. support one another in understanding the content of the lesson.
    e. listen to each other and respect one another.
- According to Johnson and Johnson (1981), there is a list of social skills that contribute to effective cooperative learning. All these skills need to be pre-taught before students participate in cooperative learning. They are:
    - **Turn-taking** - we need to teach students how to take turns when talking in a group.
    - **Respecting personal space** - students need to understand the concept of personal space and that they should not be sitting or talking too close to a person.
    - **Active listening** - Students need to learn the behaviours of active listening such as making eye-contact, nodding, encouraging the speaker, etc.
    - **Inside voices** - We teach students that inside voices is only as far as 30cm to reduce noise in the classroom. One way to do this is by telling students "If I can hear you at the front of the classroom, it means that you are not using your inside voice". It is also a behaviour management strategy.
    - **Moving safely in the classroom** - Students need to be explicitly instructed in how to move around the classroom without banging into tables and chairs and their friends.
    - **How to disagree** - Students need to be provided with scripts on how they can disagree with their group members.
    - e.g.: I hear what you are saying, but I think we can add more ideas to that.
    - **How to reach a consensus** - Teachers can create a few different actions - thumbs up/down, traffic lights, etc. to reach consensus in a group. It is important to teach that the majority always wins even if they are not correct, and you disagree. Students are learning how to behave in a democratic setting.

Positive Interdependence

- A group of students begin to see that working together allows higher chances of success.
- This success is beneficial to individuals and the group as a whole.
- Students understand that each member of their group has strengths that can allow them to contribute and participate in order to achieve success for all.
- It is further divided into nine areas.
- It is important to remember that not all nine areas can be achieved in any one lesson.
- The aim is to build up student confidence, emotional wellbeing, and awareness throughout the year.

1. Goal Interdependence

- Teachers can set goals for daily activities and tasks for students to achieve them together through cooperative learning strategies.
- These goals usually co-relate directly to the purpose of each activity or task.
- When students are in long term base groups, they can also set goals that they want to achieve together in a term or semester.

2. Role Interdependence

- Teachers allocate roles for each student in a group - this depends on the tasks and subjects. e.g.: Writer, Reader, Timekeeper, Presenter, Manager, Speaker, Director, Equipment Supervisor, etc.
- Teachers also provide clear instructions and descriptions of the roles.
- These can be printed on cards and attached to lanyards so they can be reused to help students become familiar with them over time.
- Roles ensure that every member of a group/team has a job to successfully complete.
- This also increases accountability of each role while providing overall safety in the form of cooperative learning.

Roles (this allows for differentiation):

- **WRITER:** Writes down information as group members read out their notes.
- **READER:** Reads other groups' work / reads aloud for group clarity
- **EVALUATOR:** Evaluates and determines whether the group is successfully completing the task.
- **MANAGER/TIMEKEEPER:** Keeps track of the time and manages the group (turn taking, timing, etc.)
- **EDITOR:** Edits after writing is complete.
- **PRESENTER:** Presents to the whole class.

3. **Resource Interdependence**

- Teacher provides a set of shared materials to each group.
- Students are required to share their resources with the team to complete the tasks assigned.
- In some cases, the resource given can act as a scaffold to help reduce the level of complexity of the task.
- It promotes safety and accountability and the use of various interpersonal/social skills.

4. **Incentive Interdependence**

- Teacher prepares a reward for the activity.
- Students are made aware of the reward.
- The student/pair/group that succeeds receives the reward.
- For pair and group work, this promotes a high level of cooperation,
- teamwork and improves quality of the work.
- This also creates a form of healthy competition amongst students.
- For long-term base groups, rewards may be accumulated and awarded at the end of a term.

5. **Outside Force Interdependence**

- Teachers decide how much time will be given for each of the tasks that students are doing.
- This incorporates accountability into a safe environment.
- It also ensures that students stay on task and do not have other discussions.
- It implicitly teaches time management.
- Teachers can add on time if students have not been able to complete their activities.

6. **Environmental Interdependence**

- This interdependence happens when students are required to move from their original space to a designated space to perform a task.
- The group can either move to this special meeting space on their own or it can be pre-determined by the teacher before assigning a task.
- It indirectly teaches students to move safely around the classroom and respect personal space.

7. **Identity Interdependence**

    - This is possible in short and long-term base groups.
    - Students come up with a mutual identity for the group
      e.g.: a group name, motto, logo, flag that represent their group.
    - This interdependence promotes unity and loyalty amongst team members.
    - This may be linked to a class or school reward system through the incentive interdependence.

8. **Sequence Interdependence**

    - Teacher divides the set of tasks or activities into sub-units.
    - Students have to complete the tasks in the order that has been pre-determined by the teacher.
    - The task is usually divided according to the level of difficulty, from less challenging to more challenging.
    - There will be a time factor that may influence the completion of the tasks.

9. **Simulation Interdependence**

    - Simulation is when our lesson content mirrors a real-life system or situation.
    - Simulation takes place when we bring the real world into the classrooms and ask our students to role play the situation:
      e.g.: a mock parliamentary debate, online science simulations, etc.
    - It creates understanding and awareness of systems and process.
    - It encourages students to learn and engage through the focus on analysis, problem-solving, and decision-making skills.
    - We need to include time for reflection and thought processing to allow our students to assess and share their learning experiences.
    - It can be used at any level and needs to be planned to reflect the context:
      e.g.: student age, ability level, and what the teacher wants to assess

Group Processing:

- Group Processing allows students to:

    - self-reflect and evaluate their performance as a group.
    - examine the relationship between their cooperative learning activity and their achievement as a group.
    - continuously review group sessions to explore member actions, decide which were helpful or unhelpful, and reach consensus on what actions to continue or change.
    - make decisions about their own current and future learning.

- This is more viable when teachers create and sustain long-term base groups.
- When students collaborate and cooperate in a long-term base group, they can track and monitor their improvement over a period of time, allowing for real change and success.
- Teachers can further enhance the experience by linking progress to incentives through visible improvement charts in the classroom.

The Collaborative Classroom

SPIDER WEB

Instructional Strategy	Procedure
Spider Web	1. Students form one big circle. 2. Give a ball of wool to one student. 3. The student holding the ball of wool begins. 4. Only the student holding the ball of wool is allowed to speak. 5. Pose a question. 6. The first student will attempt the question. 7. After responding, they hold the end of the woollen string and throw the ball to anyone in the circle, in any direction (refer to the image on the left). 8. Remind students to not let go of their string and only throw to someone who is not holding the woollen string. 9. The new student holding the ball of wool will attempt to answer the next question. 10. Repeat Steps 7-9 until all students are holding the wool. 11. At the end of this activity, a web will be formed, and you can see the participation of all students.
(spider web diagram of students)	
Bloom's Taxonomy Domains create / evaluate / analyse / apply / understand / remember	

SPIDER WEB

Cooperative Learning Elements	Additional Information
Safety and Individual Accountability Interpersonal/Social Skills Positive Interdependence ➢ Resource Interdependence ➢ Environmental Interdependence	**When to use** - Use as a hook to grab students' attention and put them in a receptive frame of mind. - Before a new topic – check and activate prior knowledge. - Develop students' knowledge of concepts or new learning. - Reviewing a unit either at the beginning of a new lesson or at the end of a lesson. - Before an individual assignment – writing a type of text based on a genre. - Practising new skills - supporting students to apply new skills or concepts in different contexts. **TIPS** - Predetermine the outcome of this activity: (Review lesson/reflection of the lesson, report writing, public speaking, etc). - If the class is very large, divide into groups of 10-15 and make the appropriate number of circles. - When playing with more than one group, do one group at a time. The groups waiting to play will be the audience. - Have a demonstration round if your class is playing for the first time.
Social Skills (to be pre-taught)	**Gradual Release Model**
Turn-taking Active listening Respecting personal space Moving safely in the classroom	<table><tr><td>I do</td><td>We do</td><td>You do</td></tr><tr><td>√</td><td>√</td><td>√</td></tr></table>
Online Ideas	- This activity is not viable for online learning. However, teachers can tweak and use random name spinners such as 'Wheel of Names' to teach turn-taking skills.

EXIT PASS

Instructional Strategy	Procedure
Exit Pass	1. Decide what you would like to find out about students' learning at the end of the lesson. 2. Write the question(s) on the Exit Pass (normally half the size of A4). 3. Each student receives an Exit Pass. 4. Students complete the question(s) on their Exit Pass (about 2-3 minutes). 5. Stand at the door to collect the passes as students leave the classroom. 6. Alternatively, get students to post their exit passes in a designated place in the room before leaving. 7. Examine the passes. 8. Review the question(s) at the beginning of the following lesson.
Bloom's Taxonomy Domains (create, evaluate, analyse, apply, understand, remember)	

EXIT PASS

Cooperative Learning Elements	Additional Information
Individual Accountability	**When to use** - Reviewing a unit at the end of a lesson. **TIPS** - This strategy could also be completed verbally by getting students to line up at the end of the class while the teacher stands at the door. - Students are to respond to your question(s) verbally by giving different answers from their friends. - They can also discuss with their friends before reaching you.
Social Skills (to be pre-taught)	**Gradual Release Model**
Inside voices Active listening Respecting personal space	<table><tr><th>I do</th><th>We do</th><th>You do</th></tr><tr><td></td><td></td><td>√</td></tr></table>
Online Ideas	- Teachers can upload the questions on Google Form and get students to respond before leaving.

FIND A BUDDY WHO...

Instructional Strategy	Procedure

Find a buddy who...
 	
| Find a buddy who...
	|
	|---|---|
	| **Statements** | **Buddy's name** |
	| 1) | |
	| 2) | |
	| 3) | |
	| 4) | |
	
	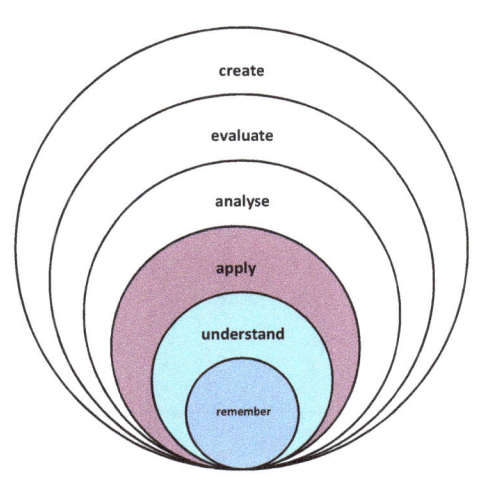
	
	Bloom's Taxonomy Domains
		1. Create a list of statements to suit the contexts of your students.
		2. Each student receives a worksheet with the list.
		    e.g.: Find a buddy who;
		    a) has travelled overseas.
		    b) has a pet at home.
		    c) is born in December.
		3. Students go through the worksheet and ask clarifying questions - new vocabulary, concepts, etc.
		4. Students practise changing statements to questions with the help of the teacher.
		    e.g. a) Have you travelled overseas?
		    b) Do you have a pet at home?
		    c) Are you born in December?
		5. Students walk around the room with their worksheets and put their hand up in search of a buddy.
		6. Students ask each buddy a question.
		    e.g.: Student A asks Student B any question from the list, and Student B responds.
		7. If the question relates to Student B and is answered, Student A writes Student B's name next to the question.
		8. If the question is not related to Student B, then they apologise by saying, "I'm sorry, this question does not relate to me".
		9. Student A asks another question.
		10. Then, student B asks Student A a question by repeating steps 5 and 6.
		11. Once done, students thank each other and raise their hands to look for another buddy.
		12. Steps 4 to 10 are repeated until students complete the sheet by finding all their buddies or until the time is up.
		13. Teacher calls out students to share their responses with the class.

FIND A BUDDY WHO...

Cooperative Learning Elements	Additional Information
Face-to-Face/Promotive Interaction Safety and Individual Accountability Interpersonal/Social Skills Positive Interdependence ➢ Outside Force Interdependence ➢ Environmental Interdependence	**When to use** • Use as a hook to grab students' attention and put them in a receptive frame of mind. • Before a new topic – check and activate prior knowledge. • Develop students' knowledge of concepts or new learning. • Reviewing a unit either at the beginning of a new lesson or at the end of a lesson. • Before an individual assignment – writing a type of text based on a genre. • Practising new skills - supporting students to apply new skills or concepts in different contexts. **TIPS** • Predetermine the outcome of this activity; (Review lesson/reflection of the lesson, report writing, public speaking, etc). • Use both inside and outside classroom areas if required. • Have a demonstration round if your class is playing for the first time.
Social Skills (to be pre-taught)	**Gradual Release Model**
Turn-taking Inside voices Active listening Respecting personal space Moving safely in the classroom	<table><tr><th>I do</th><th>We do</th><th>You do</th></tr><tr><td>√</td><td>√</td><td>√</td></tr></table>
Online Ideas	• This activity is not viable for online learning.

The Collaborative Classroom

GIVE 1 GET 1

Instructional Strategy	Procedure

Give 1 Get 1
 	
| Give 1
	Get 1 |
	|---|---|
	| | |
	| | |
	| | |
	
	Bloom's Taxonomy Domains (create, evaluate, analyse, apply, understand, remember)
		1. Pre-determine the outcome of this activity.
		   e.g.: book/movie/character review, report, persuasive text, advertisement, explanation, etc.
		2. Each student has their own piece of paper divided into two columns - Give 1, Get 1.
		3. Write question/s on board.
		   e.g.: Give 5 reasons why we should not eat fast food.
		4. Role play the activity with a student to demonstrate the process.
		5. Give time for students to process and write their own answers in the Give 1 column (5 mins) - spelling does not matter.
		6. Predetermine:
		   → how many interactions each student needs to complete (around 5 to 7).
		   → the timing for the entire activity.
		7. Give clear instructions on what they will do.
		   e.g.: Share by **giving** one idea and **getting** one idea from each classmate they are talking to.
		8. They then can walk around and talk to other students – the teacher can time this and ring a bell every 30 seconds to create flow of movement.
		9. When time is up, they come back to their desks.
		10. Give time for individual completion of work as planned.
		11. They now have a lot more information than when they started and can attempt to complete their work independently.

GIVE 1 GET 1

Cooperative Learning Elements	Additional Information
Face-to-Face/Promotive Interaction Safety and Individual Accountability Interpersonal/Social Skills Positive Interdependence ➢ Outside Force Interdependence ➢ Environmental Interdependence	**When to use** • Use as a hook to grab students' attention and put them in a receptive frame of mind. • Before a new topic – check and activate prior knowledge. • Develop students' knowledge of concepts or new learning. • Reviewing a unit either at the beginning of a new lesson or at the end of a lesson. • Before an individual assignment – writing a type of text based on a genre. • Practising new skills - supporting students to apply new skills or concepts in different contexts. **TIPS** • Predetermine numbers and timing before movement happens. • Control movement – one side of the class can be seated and the other side moving - each moving student talks to five seated students and vice versa. • Use both inside and outside classroom areas if possible.
Social Skills (to be pre-taught)	**Gradual Release Model**
Turn-taking Inside voices Active listening Respecting personal space Moving safely in the classroom	<table><tr><th>I do</th><th>We do</th><th>You do</th></tr><tr><td></td><td>√</td><td>√</td></tr></table>
Online Ideas	• This activity is not viable for online learning.

HOT POTATO

Instructional Strategy	Procedure
Hot Potato *(circle of students passing an object)* **Bloom's Taxonomy Domains** *(nested circles: create, evaluate, analyse, apply, understand, remember)*	1. Form a circle with all students. 2. Begin moving a 'potato' or any small, soft object around the circle. 3. Students are to pass the object to the person next to them. Teachers can predetermine whether this happens clockwise or anti-clockwise. 4. Have a demonstration round if your class is playing for the first time. 5. Set a timer for a random amount of time (about ten to fifteen seconds). Teachers can also use YouTube clips or music instead of timer. 6. When the timer goes off, show a flash card (or PowerPoint image) to the student holding the object. 7. The student holding the object will attempt to answer the question asked on the flash card/PowerPoint image. 8. If the answer given is correct, he/she will continue to pass the object to the person next to them. 9. If the answer is incorrect or student takes too long to answer, he/she will be out of the game and must sit outside of the circle. 10. Students are allowed to say 'Pass' twice, after which they must leave the game. 11. Repeat Steps 5-9 until you get a winner. 12. The last student standing is the winner.

HOT POTATO

Cooperative Learning Elements	Additional Information

Safety and Individual Accountability
Interpersonal/Social Skills
Positive Interdependence
   ➢ Incentive Interdependence
   ➢ Outside Force Interdependence
   ➢ Environmental Interdependence
	When to use
	- Use as a hook to grab students' attention and put them in a receptive frame of mind.
	- Before a new topic – check and activate prior knowledge.
	- Develop students' knowledge of concepts or new learning.
	- Reviewing a unit either at the beginning of a new lesson or at the end of a lesson.
	- Before an individual assignment – writing a type of text based on a genre.
	- Practising new skills - supporting students to apply new skills or concepts in different contexts.
	
	TIPS
	- For larger classes, divide students into groups of 10-15 and make the appropriate number of circles.
	- Alternatively, have a student who is the 'teacher' for each group.
	- When playing with more than one group, count 3,2,1, and have them answer together.

Social Skills (to be pre-taught)	**Gradual Release Model**
Turn-taking Inside voices Active listening Moving safely in the classroom	<table><tr><th>I do</th><th>We do</th><th>You do</th></tr><tr><td>√</td><td>√</td><td>√</td></tr></table>
Online ideas	- Teachers can use any random name picker tool available online to determine who will respond to the question. - The last name on the wheel is the winner.

INSIDE-OUTSIDE CIRCLE

Instructional Strategy	Procedure
Inside-Outside Circle OUTSIDE / INSIDE (diagram) Bloom's Taxonomy Domains (create, evaluate, analyse, apply, understand, remember)	1. Provide students with a statement: e.g.: Mobile phones should be banned at schools. 2. Allow time for students to think and make some notes. 3. Divide the class into 2 even groups; Group A will form the outside circle, and Group B will form the inside circle. 4. Students can bring along their notes. 5. Student A (outside circle) starts sharing their responses first. They are given 1 minute to do this. 6. Student B (inside circle) will demonstrate active listening skills. They are only allowed to ask clarifying questions. 7. When the time is up, Student B will share their responses. They are given 1 minute to do this. Student A will now demonstrate active listening and ask clarifying questions. 8. Once the time is up, the outside circle will move one step to the right, the inside circle will remain standing at their position. 9. Students will now share their responses with a new partner. 10. The process is repeated until each student has shared their responses with at least 5 students (pre-determined by the teacher). 11. Randomly pick a few students to report some of the findings to the class.

The Collaborative Classroom

INSIDE-OUTSIDE CIRCLE

Cooperative Learning Elements	Additional Information
Face-to-Face/Promotive Interaction Safety and Individual Accountability Interpersonal/Social Skills Positive Interdependence ➢ Outside Force Interdependence ➢ Environmental Interdependence	**When to use** • Use as a hook to grab students' attention and put them in a receptive frame of mind. • Before a new topic – check and activate prior knowledge. • Develop students' knowledge of concepts or new learning. • Reviewing a unit either at the beginning of a new lesson or at the end of a lesson. • Before an individual assignment – writing a type of text based on a genre. • Practising new skills - supporting students to apply new skills or concepts in different contexts. **TIPS** • Predetermine the outcome of this activity; (Review lesson/reflection of the lesson, report writing, public speaking, etc). • Use both inside and outside classroom areas if required.
Social Skills (to be pre-taught)	**Gradual Release Model**
Turn-taking Active Listening Inside voices Respecting personal space Moving safely in class	<table><tr><th>I do</th><th>We do</th><th>You do</th></tr><tr><td></td><td></td><td>√</td></tr></table>
Online Ideas	• This activity is not viable for online learning.

K-W-L

Instructional Strategy	Procedure
K-W-L **K-W-L** What I Know (K) | What I Want to Know (W) | What I Learned (L) Bloom's Taxonomy Domains (create, evaluate, analyse, apply, understand, remember)	1. Get students to draw a table with 3 columns into their books (as appears in the image on left). 2. Instruct students to label each column with What I Know (K), What I Want to know (W) and What I Learned (L). 3. Introduce the topic of the lesson: e.g.: 'Photosynthesis'. 4. Instruct students to independently list out everything they know about the topic in the K column (about 3-5 minutes). 5. Once completed, ask students to generate a list of questions on what additional information they want to know about the topic in the W column (about 3-5 minutes). 6. During the lesson, encourage students to look for the answers to the questions they have in the W column of the chart. 7. Allow time for students to record this new information learned in the L column. 8. Review the lesson and check if there are unanswered questions. Use these questions for further discussions.

K-W-L

Cooperative Learning Elements	Additional Information
Safety and Individual Accountability Positive Interdependence ➢ Outside Force Interdependence	**When to use** • Use as a hook to grab students' attention and put them in a receptive frame of mind. • Before a new topic – check and activate prior knowledge. • Develop students' knowledge of concepts or new learning. • Reviewing a unit either at the beginning of a new lesson or at the end of a lesson. • Before an individual assignment – writing a type of text based on a genre. **TIPS** • Predetermine the outcome of this activity; (Review lesson/reflection of the lesson, report writing, public speaking, etc). • Encourage students to keep updating the notes in the L column for the duration of the lesson (over the week). • If the questions listed by students in the 'W' column are not answered in the lesson, encourage them to search in other reference resources, such as the Internet, textbooks, etc.
Social Skills (to be pre-taught)	**Gradual Release Model**
Active Listening	<table><tr><th>I do</th><th>We do</th><th>You do</th></tr><tr><td></td><td></td><td>√</td></tr></table>
Online Ideas	• Tables in Google Docs/Google Sheets are effective options. • To monitor student engagement, teachers may ask 1-2 students to share either what they know or what they want to know about the topic.

©Boney Nathan & Seetal Kaur 2021

THINK-INK-PAIR-SHARE

Instructional Strategy	Procedure
Think-Ink-Pair-Share THINK about the question → WRITE it down PAIR with your partner SHARE your ideas with others Bloom's Taxonomy Domains (create, evaluate, analyse, apply, understand, remember)	1. Pose a specific question about a topic being discussed. e.g.: List 5 basic steps for food safety. 2. Allow wait time for students to **think** independently about what they know or have learned about the topic (about 2 minutes). 3. Allow students to write down (**ink**) their thoughts in their books (in the form of simple mind maps, words, pictures, numbers etc. (about 5 minutes). 4. **Pair** up students in the class. 5. Allow time for each student to **share** their thinking with their partner (2 minutes each). 6. Once the time is up, get each pair to share their information with another pair, small group or with the rest of the class. 7. Students can take notes while other pairs are presenting their findings.

THINK-INK-PAIR-SHARE

Cooperative Learning Elements	Additional Information
Face-to-Face/Promotive Interaction Safety and Individual Accountability Interpersonal/Social Skills Positive Interdependence ➢ Goal Interdependence ➢ Resource Interdependence ➢ Outside Force Interdependence ➢ Environmental Interdependence	**When to use** • Use as a hook to grab students' attention and put them in a receptive frame of mind. • Before a new topic – check and activate prior knowledge. • Develop students' knowledge of concepts or new learning. • Reviewing a unit either at the beginning of a new lesson or at the end of a lesson. • Before an individual assignment – writing a type of text based on a genre. • Practising new skills - supporting students to apply new skills or concepts in different contexts. **TIPS** • Predetermine the outcome of this activity: (Review lesson/reflection of the lesson, report writing, public speaking, etc). • Simply turn chairs around if space is limited.
Social Skills (to be pre-taught)	**Gradual Release Model**
Turn-taking Inside voices Active listening Respecting personal space Moving safely in the classroom	<table><tr><th>I do</th><th>We do</th><th>You do</th></tr><tr><td></td><td></td><td>√</td></tr></table>
Online Ideas	• Teachers may be able to use the breakout room feature from various online teaching platforms when students are instructed to share their thoughts in pairs or small groups.

THINK-PAIR-SHARE

Instructional Strategy	Procedure
Think-Pair-Share THINK about the question PAIR with your partner SHARE your ideas with others **Bloom's Taxonomy Domains** (create, evaluate, analyse, apply, understand, remember)	1. Pose a specific question about the topic being discussed: e.g.: List 5 characteristics of a mammal 2. Allow wait time for students to **think** independently about what they know or have learned about the topic (5 minutes). 3. **Pair** up students in the class. 4. Set time for each student to **share** their thinking with their partner (2 minutes each). 5. Once the time is up, get each pair to **share** their information with another pair, small group or with the rest of the class. 6. Students can take notes while other pairs are presenting their findings (this is dependent on what the teacher has predetermined as the purpose of the lesson).

THINK-PAIR-SHARE

Cooperative Learning Elements	Additional Information
Face-to-Face/Promotive Interaction Safety and Individual Accountability Interpersonal/Social Skills Positive Interdependence ➢ Goal Interdependence ➢ Outside Force Interdependence ➢ Environmental Interdependence	**When to use**<ul><li>Use as a hook to grab students' attention and put them in a receptive frame of mind.</li><li>Before a new topic – check and activate prior knowledge.</li><li>Develop students' knowledge of concepts or new learning.</li><li>Reviewing a unit either at the beginning of a new lesson or at the end of a lesson.</li><li>Before an individual assignment – writing a type of text based on a genre.</li><li>Practising new skills - supporting students to apply new skills or concepts in different contexts.</li></ul>**TIPS**<ul><li>Predetermine the purpose of this activity; (Review lesson/reflection of the lesson, report writing, public speaking, etc).</li><li>Simply turn chairs around if space is limited.</li></ul>
Social Skills (to be pre-taught)	**Gradual Release Model**
Turn-taking Inside voices Active listening Respecting personal space Moving safely in the classroom	<table><tr><th>I do</th><th>We do</th><th>You do</th></tr><tr><td></td><td></td><td>√</td></tr></table>
Online Ideas	<ul><li>Teachers may be able to use the breakout room feature from various online teaching platforms when students are instructed to work in pairs or small groups.</li></ul>

The Collaborative Classroom

TURN AND TALK

Instructional Strategy	Procedure

Turn and Talk	1. Each student is given a piece of paper with a statement and space to jot down ideas.
	   e.g.: Mobile phones must not be allowed in schools.
	   You should be able to get your driver's licence at the age of 15.
	2. Check for understanding.
	3. Students write down their views (about 2-3 minutes).
	4. Students turn to their partners to share their ideas.
	5. Student A - provides their opinions.
	   Student B - takes notes.
	6. They switch and the process is repeated.
	7. The whole process takes about 5 minutes.
	8. Students then turn around for a new partner and repeat steps 5-6.
	9. Students are not moving around the classroom. They are simply turning around and talking to students sitting near them.
	10. The activity continues until students have gathered a list of 4 different views.
	11. Teacher may ask 2-3 students to share their discussions.

Bloom's Taxonomy Domains (create, evaluate, analyse, apply, understand, remember)	

The Collaborative Classroom 25

TURN AND TALK

Cooperative Learning Elements	Additional Information
Face-to-Face/Promotive Interaction Safety and Individual Accountability Interpersonal/Social Skills Positive Interdependence ➢ Goal Interdependence ➢ Resource Interdependence ➢ Outside Force Interdependence ➢ Environmental Interdependence	**When to use** • Use as a hook to grab students' attention and put them in a receptive frame of mind. • Before a new topic – check and activate prior knowledge. • Develop students' knowledge of concepts or new learning. • Reviewing a unit either at the beginning of a new lesson or at the end of a lesson. • Before an individual assignment – writing a type of text based on a genre. • Practising new skills - supporting students to apply new skills or concepts in different contexts. **TIPS** • Have a demonstration round if your class is playing for the first time.
Social Skills (to be pre-taught)	**Gradual Release Model**
Turn-taking Inside voices Active listening Respecting personal space Moving safely in the classroom	<table><tr><th>I do</th><th>We do</th><th>You do</th></tr><tr><td>√</td><td>√</td><td>√</td></tr></table>
Online Ideas	• This activity is not viable for online learning.

TWO-MINUTE INTERVIEW

Instructional Strategy	Procedure
Two-Minute Interview A B Bloom's Taxonomy Domains (create, evaluate, analyse, apply, understand, remember)	1. Based on the topic of discussion, get each student to come up with a list of questions. 2. Alternatively, teacher can present a list of questions for the whole class. e.g.: Effects of air pollution 3. Check for understanding. 4. Divide the class in half. 5. Students stand in two long rows facing each other. 6. Label one row as 'A' and the opposite row as 'B'. Row A- **INTERVIEWER** ➤ asks questions on their lists and listen actively to the comments and thoughts of the interviewee, paraphrasing key points and significant details. Row B- **INTERVIEWEE** ➤ responds to the questions 7. Allow 2 minutes for this process to happen. 8. Once the time is up, students switch roles: Student A- **INTERVIEWEE** Student B- **INTERVIEWER** 9. After one round of interviews, students in Row A move one step to the left so that everyone has a new partner. 10. Students need to talk to at least 5 peers to gather enough evidence to generate a full-class discussion.

TWO-MINUTE INTERVIEW

Cooperative Learning Elements	Additional Information
Face-to-Face/Promotive Interaction Safety and Individual Accountability Interpersonal/Social Skills Positive Interdependence ➤ Goal Interdependence ➤ Role Interdependence ➤ Resource Interdependence ➤ Outside Force Interdependence ➤ Environmental Interdependence	**When to use** - Use as a hook to grab students' attention and put them in a receptive frame of mind. - Before a new topic – check and activate prior knowledge. - Develop students' knowledge of concepts or new learning. - Reviewing a unit either at the beginning of a new lesson or at the end of a lesson. - Before an individual assignment – writing a type of text based on a genre. - Practising new skills - supporting students to apply new skills or concepts in different contexts. **TIPS** - Predetermine the outcome of this activity; (Review lesson/reflection of the lesson, report writing, public speaking, etc). - If there are odd number of students: ➤ the teacher can join in the activity. ➤ assign one student to be the timekeeper. After the first round of interview, this student will be replaced by another student. - The last student A will move to the front of the new row when the movement happens.
Social Skills (to be pre-taught)	**Gradual Release Model**
Turn-taking Inside voices Active listening Respecting personal space Moving safely in the classroom	<table><tr><th>I do</th><th>We do</th><th>You do</th></tr><tr><td>√</td><td>√</td><td>√</td></tr></table>
Online Ideas	- This activity is not viable for online learning.

The Collaborative Classroom

WORD WALL

Instructional Strategy	Procedure
Word Wall **Positive feeling adjectives** | Excited	Enthusiastic
Happy	Passionate
Cheerful	Courteous
Clever	Comical
Confident	Grateful
Respectable	Reliable
Kind	Earnest
Honest	Friendly | *(Bloom's Taxonomy Domains diagram: create, evaluate, analyse, apply, understand, remember)* **Bloom's Taxonomy Domains**	1. This is an effective activity to expand students' vocabulary. 2. Put up a piece of butcher's paper on a wall. 3. Write a word or a phrase in the middle or at the top of the paper (refer to the image on the left). 4. Get students to write around or under the word or phrase. e.g.: synonyms, antonyms, adjectives, etc. 5. Students add their initials to their responses. 6. Once everyone has contributed, the teacher collects the butcher's paper, types out the correct responses, and adds the list to the existing class word wall.

WORD WALL

Cooperative Learning Elements	Additional Information
Face-to-Face/Promotive Interaction Safety and Individual Accountability Interpersonal/Social Skills Positive Interdependence ➢ Goal Interdependence ➢ Resource Interdependence ➢ Outside Force Interdependence ➢ Environmental Interdependence	**When to use**<ul><li>Use as a hook to grab students' attention and put them in a receptive frame of mind.</li><li>Before a new topic – check and activate prior knowledge.</li><li>Develop students' knowledge of concepts or new learning.</li><li>Reviewing a unit either at the beginning of a new lesson or at the end of a lesson.</li><li>Before an individual assignment – writing a type of text based on a genre.</li><li>Practising new skills - supporting students to apply new skills or concepts in different contexts.</li></ul>**TIPS**<ul><li>Predetermine the outcome of this activity (Review lesson/reflection of the lesson, report writing, etc).</li><li>Predetermine numbers and timing before movement happens.</li><li>To manage movement, release small groups of 5 at a time (about 1 minute).</li><li>For large class sizes, students can either work in pairs or groups.</li></ul>
Social Skills (to be pre-taught)	**Gradual Release Model**
Turn-taking Inside voices Active listening Respecting personal space Moving safely in the classroom	<table><tr><th>I do</th><th>We do</th><th>You do</th></tr><tr><td></td><td></td><td>√</td></tr></table>
Online Ideas	<ul><li>A table can be uploaded onto Google Doc/Google Sheets, with the word written at the top. Teachers can see students typing their answers and adding on ideas.</li></ul>

ABC SUMMARY

Instructional Strategy	Procedure
ABC Summary	1. Each student in the class is assigned a letter of the alphabet. 2. Pre-determine student activity. (Have a demonstration round if your class is doing this activity for the first time.) e.g.: Watch a video segment, listen to an audio file, listen to the teacher reading out loud, discuss a poster, etc. 3. Pause frequently and allow time for students to take notes. 4. Repeat Step 2. 5. Students are asked to summarise what they watched/listened using the letter they have been given – e.g.: This video **allows** us to… This video **begins** with… This video **changed** my… 6. Teacher will scribe/type the summaries. 7. All the summaries are collated and edited to produce one good example for the class.
Bloom's Taxonomy Domains (create, evaluate, analyse, apply, understand, remember)	

The Collaborative Classroom

ABC SUMMARY

Cooperative Learning Elements	Additional Information
Face-to-Face/Promotive Interaction Safety and Individual Accountability Interpersonal/Social Skills Positive Interdependence ➢ Goal Interdependence ➢ Environmental Interdependence	**When to use** • Use as a hook to grab students' attention and put them in a receptive frame of mind. • Before a new topic – check and activate prior knowledge. • Develop students' knowledge of concepts or new learning. • Reviewing a unit either at the beginning of a new lesson or at the end of a lesson. • Before an individual assignment – writing a type of text based on a genre. • Practising new skills - supporting students to apply new skills or concepts in different contexts. **TIPS** • Predetermine the outcome of this activity; (Review lesson/reflection of the lesson, report writing, public speaking, etc). • Simply turn chairs around if space is limited. • Additional support can be given by allowing students small group discussion time before sharing with the whole class. • This can also be done in letter pairs – 2 students work together and are assigned the same letter.
Social Skills (to be pre-taught)	**Gradual Release Model**
Turn-taking Inside voices Active listening Respecting personal space Moving safely in the classroom How to disagree How to reach a consensus	<table><tr><th>I do</th><th>We do</th><th>You do</th></tr><tr><td>√</td><td>√</td><td>√</td></tr></table>
Online Ideas	• Tables in Google Docs/Google Sheets are effective options for students to share their summaries. • This is an effective online activity for individual student work.

CHUNKING

Instructional Strategy	Procedure

Chunking
 	
Bloom's Taxonomy Domains (create, evaluate, analyse, apply, understand, remember)
	1. Divide students into small groups of 3-4.
	2. Provide them with different paragraphs from a text – it could a text that you are planning to introduce or one that you have already started to read.
	3. Provide a decoding strategy rubric: e.g.:
	    ➤ Circle new or unfamiliar words
	    ➤ Use commas, brackets etc. to guess what a word or phrase means
	    ➤ Underline important information
	4. Ask students to discuss their paragraphs.
	5. Students need to rewrite their paragraphs using their own words.
	6. They will be asked to share this with the whole class to share understanding of the whole text.
	7. Alternative ideas for this strategy:
	    ➤ You can provide students with a graphic organiser to help them chunk their thoughts and ideas.
	    ➤ Start slow – if it the first time, students can work as whole class and just focus on identifying and understanding main words.
	    ➤ Differentiate – start with chunking phrases for some of your students.
	    ➤ Students can also chunk their information into a picture.
	    ➤ You may provide questions to prompt.
	    ➤ You can use the **Jigsaw** strategy in conjunction with **Chunking**.

CHUNKING

Cooperative Learning Elements	Additional Information
Face-to-Face/Promotive Interaction Safety and Individual Accountability Interpersonal/Social Skills Positive Interdependence ➢ Goal Interdependence ➢ Resource Interdependence ➢ Outside Force Interdependence ➢ Environmental Interdependence	**When to use** • Before a new topic – check and activate prior knowledge. • Develop students' knowledge of concepts or new learning. • Reviewing a unit either at the beginning of a new lesson or at the end of a lesson. • Before an individual assignment – writing a type of text based on a genre. • Practising new skills - supporting students to apply new skills or concepts in different contexts. **TIPS** • Simply turn chairs around if space is limited. • Use both inside and outside classroom areas if required. • You can do this as a whole class using one paragraph at a time – students can work with the person sitting next to them.
Social Skills (to be pre-taught)	**Gradual Release Model**
Turn-taking Inside voices Active listening Respecting personal space Moving safely in the classroom How to disagree How to reach a consensus	<table><tr><th>I do</th><th>We do</th><th>You do</th></tr><tr><td>√</td><td>√</td><td>√</td></tr></table>
Online Ideas	• Tables in Google Docs/Google Sheets are effective options. • Teachers may be able to use the breakout room feature from various online teaching platforms when students are instructed to work in pairs or small groups.

DICTIONARY LOOP

Instructional Strategy	Procedure
Dictionary Loop Bloom's Taxonomy Domains	1. Put students in small groups of 3-4. 2. Teacher models the task with the whole class. 3. Each group receives a dictionary and a card. 4. The cards may be different for each group. 5. The card has the first letter of a word and its definition/description underneath. e.g.: WORD : S _ _ _ _ _ DEFINITION: an institution for educating children 6. Students use the dictionary to work out what the word is. 7. Once students get the answer, they check with the teacher. 8. If the answer given is correct, teacher hands out the next card. The next card will begin with the last letter of the previous card. e.g.: SCHOOL → 'L' 9. If the answer is incorrect, the teacher may give a clue (second letter of the word) or encourage students to keep trying. 10. The activity loops and continues until the final word links back to the original letter 'S'. e.g.: **S**CHOOL – LETTER – ROSE – EAST - TOS**S** 11. The first group to complete the game may be rewarded.

The Collaborative Classroom

DICTIONARY LOOP

Cooperative Learning Elements	Additional Information

Face-to-Face/Promotive Interaction
Safety and Individual Accountability
Interpersonal/Social Skills
Positive Interdependence
   ➢ Goal Interdependence
   ➢ Resource Interdependence
   ➢ Incentive Interdependence
   ➢ Outside Force Interdependence
   ➢ Environmental Interdependence
   ➢ Sequence Interdependence
	When to use
	• Use as a hook to grab students' attention and put them in a receptive frame of mind.
	• Before a new topic – check and activate prior knowledge.
	• Develop students' knowledge of concepts or new learning.
	• Reviewing a unit either at the beginning of a new lesson or at the end of a lesson.
	• Before an individual assignment – writing a type of text based on a genre.
	• Practising new skills - supporting students to apply new skills or concepts in different contexts.
	TIPS
	• Predetermine the outcome of this activity; (Spelling test/review lesson/reflection of the lesson, report writing, public speaking, etc).
	• Advanced students could do this activity independently.

Social Skills (to be pre-taught)	**Gradual Release Model**
Turn-taking Inside voices Active listening Respecting personal space Moving safely in the classroom How to disagree How to reach a consensus	<table><tr><th>I do</th><th>We do</th><th>You do</th></tr><tr><td>√</td><td>√</td><td>√</td></tr></table>
Online Ideas	• Teachers can upload the list onto Google Docs. Students can use online dictionaries. • Teachers may be able to use the breakout room feature from various online teaching platforms when students are instructed to work in pairs or small groups.

PLACEMAT

Instructional Strategy	Procedure
Placemat *(Placemat diagrams shown for different group sizes)* **Bloom's Taxonomy Domains** *(concentric circles: create, evaluate, analyse, apply, understand, remember)*	1. Group student in small groups of 2, 3, or a maximum of 4. 2. Distribute ONE A3 paper to each group. 3. Students will draw a placemat (refer to the image on the left) according to the number of students in the group. This is modelled by the teacher. 4. Write question/s or a topic on the board. e.g.: Question may be -How do you prevent from getting Covid-19? OR a topic may be - Covid-19. 5. Set an amount of time for students to write down their thoughts (3-5 minutes). 6. All students write at the same time. 7. Let students know that they can write in any direction but only in their own spaces. 8. Students can use different coloured pens or write their initials in their spaces. 9. Silent activity - Students are not allowed to speak or discuss at this point and spelling does not matter. 10. After the time is up, give students another 5 minutes to discuss and come up with a consensus to write in the middle section of the paper. 11. Adjust time to context – difficulty of question, student level, etc. 12. After discussion time is over, they share their consensus with the whole class.

PLACEMAT

Cooperative Learning Elements	Additional Information

Face-to-Face/Promotive Interaction
Safety and Individual Accountability
Interpersonal/Social Skills
Positive Interdependence
   ➢ Goal Interdependence
   ➢ Resource Interdependence
   ➢ Outside Force Interdependence
   ➢ Environmental Interdependence
	When to use
	• Use as a hook to grab students' attention and put them in a receptive frame of mind.
	• Before a new topic – check and activate prior knowledge.
	• Develop students' knowledge of concepts or new learning.
	• Reviewing a unit either at the beginning of a new lesson or at the end of a lesson.
	• Before an individual assignment – writing a type of text based on a genre.
	• Practising new skills - supporting students to apply new skills or concepts in different contexts.
	
	TIPS
	• Simply turn chairs around if space is limited.
	• Teachers can assign two different questions to different groups OR each group could have a different question based on the same topic they are learning.

Social Skills (to be pre-taught)	**Gradual Release Model**
Turn-taking Inside voices Active listening Respecting personal space How to disagree How to reach a consensus	<table><tr><th>I do</th><th>We do</th><th>You do</th></tr><tr><td></td><td>√</td><td>√</td></tr></table>
Online Ideas	• Teachers may be able to use the breakout room feature via various online teaching platforms. • Tables in Google Docs/Google Sheets are effective options.

The Collaborative Classroom

ROUND ROBIN

Instructional Strategy	Procedure
Round Robin Bloom's Taxonomy Domains (create, evaluate, analyse, apply, understand, remember)	1. This is a good brainstorming activity. 2. Put students in groups of 4-6. 3. Number each student; 1, 2, 3, 4, 5, 6 - this will help with turn-taking. 4. Appoint 1 student from each group to be the RECORDER. The RECORDER does not have to contribute to the discussion. 5. Teacher will pose a question/idea: e.g.: What can we do to stay safe during Covid-19? 6. Students take turns starting from number 1 to contribute to the discussion. 7. The RECORDER from each group will record the answers from the discussion. 8. All the RECORDERs will share their notes with the rest of the class. 9. Students can now return to their places and continue working individually or in pairs to complete what has been pre-determined by the teacher - essay, genre writing tasks, etc.

ROUND ROBIN

Cooperative Learning Elements	Additional Information
Face-to-Face/Promotive Interaction Safety and Individual Accountability Interpersonal/Social Skills Positive Interdependence ➢ Goal Interdependence ➢ Role Interdependence ➢ Outside Force Interdependence ➢ Environmental Interdependence	**When to use** • Before a new topic – check and activate prior knowledge. • Develop students' knowledge of concepts or new learning. • Reviewing a unit either at the beginning of a new lesson or at the end of a lesson. • Before an individual assignment – writing a type of text based on a genre. • Practising new skills - supporting students to apply new skills or concepts in different contexts. **TIPS** • Predetermine the outcome of this activity: (Review lesson/reflection of the lesson, report writing, public speaking, etc.). • Simply turn chairs around if space is limited. • Use both inside and outside classroom areas if required. • Predetermine numbers and timing before movement happens.
Social Skills (to be pre-taught)	**Gradual Release Model**
Turn-taking Inside voices Active listening Respecting personal space Moving safely in the classroom	<table><tr><th>I do</th><th>We do</th><th>You do</th></tr><tr><td></td><td></td><td>√</td></tr></table>
Online Ideas	• Teachers may be able to use the breakout room feature from various online teaching platforms when students are instructed to work in pairs or small groups. • The RECORDER can present to the rest of the class via various online learning platforms.

©Boney Nathan & Seetal Kaur 2021

SCAVENGER HUNT

Instructional Strategy	Procedure
Scavenger Hunt Bloom's Taxonomy Domains	1. Divide class into small groups/teams of 3 to 4 students. 2. Each team is given a list (refer to the example on page 43). 3. Teacher decides what to put on the list depending on classroom context – ensure that most things on the list are either available or substitutable by the students. 4. Go over instructions and model to ensure students are clear about the task. 5. Check for understanding – ask questions. 6. Put timer on (10 minutes maximum). 7. Students start looking for the items on the list. 8. They also fill in the form – the **Writer** can be pre-determined. 9. Students tally up points when time is up. 10. Teacher can pre-determine a prize for the winners (e.g.: extra computer time, linked to classroom/school award system, etc.).

The Collaborative Classroom

SCAVENGER HUNT

Cooperative Learning Elements	Additional Information

Face-to-Face/Promotive Interaction
Safety and Individual Accountability
Interpersonal/Social Skills
Positive Interdependence
    ➢ Goal Interdependence
    ➢ Role Interdependence
    ➢ Resource Interdependence
    ➢ Incentive Interdependence
    ➢ Outside Force Interdependence
    ➢ Environmental Interdependence
	When to use
	• Use as a hook to grab students' attention and put them in a receptive frame of mind.
	• Before a new topic – check and activate prior knowledge.
	
	TIPS
	• Pre-set home group stations for the rest of term/semester.
	• Use both inside and outside classroom areas if possible.
	• Simply turn chairs around if space is limited.

Social Skills (to be pre-taught)	**Gradual Release Model**
Turn-taking Inside voices Active listening Respecting personal space How to disagree How to reach a consensus	<table><tr><th>I do</th><th>We do</th><th>You do</th></tr><tr><td></td><td>√</td><td>√</td></tr></table>
Online Ideas	• Teachers may be able to use the breakout room feature via various online teaching platforms. • Teachers can upload the list onto Google Docs. • Students will need to show evidence of swaps – they can just hold them up to the camera.

SCAVENGER HUNT INSTRUCTIONS

Scavenger Hunt Instructions:

1. Your team needs to collect all the item on the list.
2. Each item you gather will give you 2 points.
3. You are not allowed to move around the classroom – look for the items in your bags, pencil cases etc.
4. You are allowed to substitute or swap item – for example, you can swap a yellow highlighter with a pink one.
5. You will get 1 point for the swap.
6. You have 10 minutes when I say "GO".
7. The team with the most point will win.

	Object	Substitute	Points
1.	Blue pen		
2.	Lipstick		
3.	Photo		
4.	Library card		
5.	Green highlighter		
6.	Chocolate		
7.	USB		
8.	Hair tie		
9.	Water bottle		
10.	Necktie		
11.	Notebook		
12.	Story book		
13.	Money		
14.	Sunglasses		
15.	Phone		

SCAVENGER HUNT INSTRUCTIONS

Scavenger Hunt Instructions:

1. Your team needs to collect all the item on the list.
2. Each item you gather will give you 2 points.
3. You are not allowed to move around the classroom – look for the items in your bags, pencil cases etc.
4. You are allowed to substitute or swap item – for example, you can swap a yellow highlighter with a pink one.
5. You will get 1 point for the swap.
6. You have 10 minutes when I say "GO".
7. The team with the most point will win.

	Object	**Substitute**	**Points**
1.			
2.			
3.			
4.			
5.			
6.			
7.			
8.			
9.			
10.			
11.			
12.			
13.			
14.			
15.			

TALKING STICK

Instructional Strategy	Procedure
Talking Stick	1. This is an effective listening and speaking activity. 2. Group students in small groups of 2-4. 3. Give each group a stick – this will be passed around clockwise or anticlockwise – predetermined by the teacher. 4. Teacher will pose a question or a topic for discussion. 5. Teacher will model the process with a small group. 6. Only the student holding the stick is allowed to speak – all other students will listen actively. 7. Students are allowed to agree or disagree with their peers. 8. When all the students have had their turn, they can share their group discussion with the whole class.
Bloom's Taxonomy Domains (create, evaluate, analyse, apply, understand, remember)	

The Collaborative Classroom

TALKING STICK

Cooperative Learning Elements	Additional Information

Face-to-Face/Promotive Interaction
Safety and Individual Accountability
Interpersonal/Social Skills
Positive Interdependence
    ➢ Resource Interdependence
    ➢ Outside Force Interdependence
    ➢ Environmental Interdependence
	When to use
	• Use as a hook to grab students' attention and put them in a receptive frame of mind.
	• Before a new topic – check and activate prior knowledge.
	• Develop students' knowledge of concepts or new learning.
	• Reviewing a unit either at the beginning of a new lesson or at the end of a lesson.
	• Before an individual assignment – writing a type of text based on a genre.
	• Practising new skills - supporting students to apply new skills or concepts in different contexts.
	TIPS
	• For larger classes, create one big classroom circle instead of a few small circles.
	• Use both inside and outside classroom areas if required.
	• Teacher can assign different questions to different smaller groups OR each group could have a different question based on the same topic they are learning.
	• This is also a behaviour management tool that can be used during mat time in a primary classroom.

Social Skills (to be pre-taught)	**Gradual Release Model**
Turn-taking Inside voices Active listening Respecting personal space Moving safely in the classroom How to disagree	<table><tr><th>I do</th><th>We do</th><th>You do</th></tr><tr><td>√</td><td>√</td><td>√</td></tr></table>
Online Ideas	• Teachers can use any random name picker tool available online to determine who will respond to the question.

TEAM PAIR SOLO

Instructional Strategy	Procedure
Team Pair Solo Bloom's Taxonomy Domains (create, evaluate, analyse, apply, understand, remember)	1. Group students into teams of four or more (depending on the size of the class). 2. Each group is given a problem to solve (about 10 minutes). 3. Once the time is up, check the answer. 4. If the answer is incorrect, provide extra time for discussion (about 5 minutes). 5. If the answer is correct, break the team to form pairs. 6. Each pair is given a new problem (extension from the first problem) to solve (about 5 minutes). 7. Once the time is up, check the answer. 8. If the answer is incorrect, provide extra time for discussion (about 2 minutes). 9. If the answer is correct, break the pair for students to work independently. 10. Each student is given a new problem to solve. 11. Students are to use the skills gathered from their discussion in groups and pairs to solve their problem (about 5 minutes). 12. Once the time is up, check the responses for the whole class.

TEAM PAIR SOLO

Cooperative Learning Elements	Additional Information
Face-to-Face/Promotive Interaction Safety and Individual Accountability Interpersonal/Social Skills Positive Interdependence ➢ Goal Interdependence ➢ Resource Interdependence ➢ Outside Force Interdependence ➢ Environmental Interdependence	**When to use** • Use as a hook to grab students' attention and put them in a receptive frame of mind. • Before a new topic – check and activate prior knowledge. • Develop students' knowledge of concepts or new learning. • Reviewing a unit either at the beginning of a new lesson or at the end of a lesson. • Before an individual assignment – writing a type of text based on a genre. • Practising new skills - supporting students to apply new skills or concepts in different contexts. **TIPS** • Predetermine the outcome of this activity; (Review lesson/reflection of the lesson, report writing, public speaking, etc). • Simply turn chairs around if space is limited.
Social Skills (to be pre-taught)	**Gradual Release Model**
Turn-taking Inside voices Active listening Respecting personal space Moving safely in the classroom How to disagree How to reach a consensus	<table><tr><th>I do</th><th>We do</th><th>You do</th></tr><tr><td></td><td>√</td><td>√</td></tr></table>
Online Ideas	• Teachers can upload the questions onto Google Docs. • Teachers may be able to use the breakout room feature from various online teaching platforms when students are instructed to work in pairs or small groups.

THREE-STEP INTERVIEW

Instructional Strategy	Procedure
Three-Step Interview Pair A — Student A, Student B Pair B — Student A, Student B Each pair share their ideas **individually** **Bloom's Taxonomy Domains** (create, evaluate, analyse, apply, understand, remember)	1. Predetermine the outcome of this activity: (Review lesson/reflection of the lesson, report writing, public speaking, etc). 2. Pose a specific issue about the topic being discussed: e.g.: Effects of air pollution 3. Create a set of guiding questions regarding the topic. 4. Check for understanding. 5. Put students in pairs: Student A- **INTERVIEWER** → Asks probing questions and listens actively to the comments and thoughts of the interviewee, paraphrasing key points and significant details. Student B- **INTERVIEWEE** → answers questions from interviewer. 6. Allow about 2 minutes for this process to happen. 7. Once the time is up, students switch roles; Student A- **INTERVIEWEE**, Student B- **INTERVIEWER**. 8. After one round of interviews, instruct pairs to find another pair and form groups of four. 9. Students take turns to individually summarise what they have gathered from the interviews (about 1 minute each). 10. The other students in the group can take notes at this stage.

THREE-STEP INTERVIEW

Cooperative Learning Elements	Additional Information
Face-to-Face/Promotive Interaction Safety and Individual Accountability Interpersonal/Social Skills Positive Interdependence ➢ Goal Interdependence ➢ Role Interdependence ➢ Resource Interdependence ➢ Outside Force Interdependence ➢ Environmental Interdependence	**When to use** • Use as a hook to grab students' attention and put them in a receptive frame of mind. • Before a new topic – check and activate prior knowledge. • Develop students' knowledge of concepts or new learning. • Reviewing a unit either at the beginning of a new lesson or at the end of a lesson. • Before an individual assignment – writing a type of text based on a genre. • Practising new skills - supporting students to apply new skills or concepts in different contexts. **TIPS** • Adjust time according to student levels and context. • Simply turn chairs around if space is limited. • If there are odd number of students, they can work in groups of threes.
Social Skills (to be pre-taught)	**Gradual Release Model**
Turn-taking Inside voices Active listening Respecting personal space Moving safely in the classroom	<table><tr><th>I do</th><th>We do</th><th>You do</th></tr><tr><td>√</td><td>√</td><td>√</td></tr></table>
Online Ideas	• Teachers can upload the topic onto Google Docs. • Teachers may be able to use the breakout room feature from various online teaching platforms when students are instructed to work in pairs or small groups. • Students may be able to collaborate and present their findings via various online learning platforms.

3-2-1 STRATEGY

Instructional Strategy	Procedure
3-2-1 Strategy 3 things discoverd 2 things that interest me 1 Question I still have **Bloom's Taxonomy Domains** (create, evaluate, analyse, apply, understand, remember)	1. This strategy is used at the end of a lesson. 2. At the start of the lesson, let students know that they will be asked to reflect on what they have learnt. 3. At the end of the lesson: → Students individually or in pairs list as many key ideas that they have learnt from the lesson (3-5 minutes). → Out of those key ideas, students highlight **three** things they have discovered from the lesson (2 minutes). → Once completed, students circle **two** things that interest them the most (2 minutes). → Students then write down **1** question that has not been answered in the lesson (2 minutes). 4. Collate the questions from all students. 5. Address these questions in the following lesson.

The Collaborative Classroom

3-2-1 STRATEGY

Cooperative Learning Elements	Additional Information
Face-to-Face/Promotive Interaction Safety and Individual Accountability Interpersonal/Social Skills Positive Interdependence ➢ Goal Interdependence ➢ Outside Force Interdependence ➢ Environmental Interdependence	**When to use** • Reviewing a unit at the end of a lesson. • Before an individual assignment – writing a type of text based on a genre. • Practising new skills - supporting students to apply new skills or concepts in different contexts. **TIPS** • Predetermine the outcome of this activity; (Review lesson/reflection of the lesson, report writing, public speaking, etc). • Simply turn chairs around if space is limited. • Higher-level students can complete this activity individually.
Social Skills (to be pre-taught)	**Gradual Release Model**
Turn-taking Inside voices Active listening Respecting personal space	<table><tr><th>I do</th><th>We do</th><th>You do</th></tr><tr><td></td><td></td><td>√</td></tr></table>
Online Ideas	• Tables in Google Docs/Google Sheets are effective options for student response. • Students may be able to collaborate and present their reflection via various online learning platforms.

AGREEMENT CIRCLES

Instructional Strategy	Procedure
Agreement Circles Bloom's Taxonomy Domains	1. Students stand in a large circle. 2. Teacher reads the first statement. 3. Students are given 5-10 seconds to think about the statement. 4. Students who agree with the statement are asked to move to the centre of the circle and students who disagree stay outside. 5. Match students who agree with students who disagree – the proportion depends on the numbers that you have. 6. Give students 5-7 minutes to have a discussion and defend their opinions by justifying why they agree or disagree. 7. When time is up, read the statement again to see if any of the students have changed their minds. 8. They move to the agree group inside the circle or the disagree group outside the circle. 9. You can restart the process with a new statement.

The Collaborative Classroom   53

AGREEMENT CIRCLES

Cooperative Learning Elements	Additional Information
Face-to-Face/Promotive Interaction Safety and Individual Accountability Interpersonal/Social Skills Positive Interdependence: ➢ Outside Force Interdependence ➢ Environmental Interdependence	**When to use**<ul><li>Use as a hook to grab students' attention and put them in a receptive frame of mind.</li><li>Before a new topic – check and activate prior knowledge.</li><li>Develop students' knowledge of concepts or new learning.</li><li>Reviewing a unit either at the beginning of a new lesson or at the end of a lesson.</li><li>Before an individual assignment – writing a type of text based on a genre.</li><li>Practising new skills - supporting students to apply new skills or concepts in different contexts.</li></ul>**TIPS**<ul><li>Predetermine the outcome of this activity; (Review lesson/reflection of the lesson, report writing, public speaking, etc).</li><li>For large classes, divide into groups of 10-15 and make the appropriate number of circles - each group could have a different question.</li><li>Alternatively, have a student who is the 'teacher' for each group.</li><li>Have a demonstration round if your class is playing for the first time.</li></ul>
Social Skills (to be pre-taught)	**Gradual Release Model**
Turn-taking Inside voices Active listening Respecting personal space Moving safely in the classroom How to disagree	<table><tr><th>I do</th><th>We do</th><th>You do</th></tr><tr><td>√</td><td>√</td><td>√</td></tr></table>
Online Ideas	<ul><li>This activity is not viable for online learning. However, teachers can tweak and use random name spinners such as 'Wheel of Names', to teach turn-taking skills.</li></ul>

ASK-N-SWITCH

Instructional Strategy	Procedure

Ask-n-Switch
 	
switch
 	
Bloom's Taxonomy Domains
(create, evaluate, analyse, apply, understand, remember)
	1. Divide the class into 2 groups – A and B.
	2. Prepare 2 sets of cards: Set A and Set B.
	3. On each set:
	   → Question about a topic they have learnt on one side.
	   → Question + answer on the other side.
	4. Provide each student with a card.
	5. Get students to line up – Group A facing Group B.
	6. A holds up their question to B and reads the question.
	7. When B answers, A will:
	   → say "Good answer, you are correct." if the answer is correct.
	   → support and encourage by saying "Don't give up / Keep trying, you're almost there etc." if incorrect.
	8. Now roles will reverse, and B will ask their question to A.
	9. Student B will repeat Step 7.
	10. Time the whole process – maybe around 2-3 minutes for each pair.
	11. When time is up, they thank each other, exchange their cards, and move one step to left or right as pre-determined by the teacher.
	12. Teacher walks around and facilitates the process and encourages students to stay task.
	13. Steps 6-11 are repeated with a new partner and new cards.
	14. Total time for the process is pre-determined by the teacher.
	   e.g.: 20 minutes of a lesson, the whole lesson, etc.

The Collaborative Classroom

ASK-N-SWITCH

Cooperative Learning Elements	Additional Information
Face-to-Face/Promotive Interaction Safety and Individual Accountability Interpersonal/Social Skills Positive Interdependence ➢ Resource Interdependence ➢ Outside Force Interdependence ➢ Environmental Interdependence	**When to use** • Use as a hook to grab students' attention and put them in a receptive frame of mind. • Before a new topic – check and activate prior knowledge. • Develop students' knowledge of concepts or new learning. • Reviewing a unit either at the beginning of a new lesson or at the end of a lesson. • Before an individual assignment – writing a type of text based on a genre. • Practising new skills - supporting students to apply new skills or concepts in different contexts. **TIPS** • Predetermine the outcome of this activity; (Review lesson/reflection of the lesson, report writing, public speaking, etc). • Use both inside and outside classroom areas if required. • Have a demonstration round if your class is playing for the first time.
Social Skills (to be pre-taught)	**Gradual Release Model**
Turn-taking Inside voices Active listening Respecting personal space Moving safely in the classroom	<table><tr><th>I do</th><th>We do</th><th>You do</th></tr><tr><td>√</td><td>√</td><td>√</td></tr></table>
Online Ideas	• Students come prepared for their online lesson with their own questions. • Student picks a classmate to answer their question and uses the correct/incorrect script to provide feedback. • The student who answers then asks their question and picks another classmate.

CONCEPT ATTAINMENT

Instructional Strategy	Procedure
Concept Attainment YES Examples / NO Examples 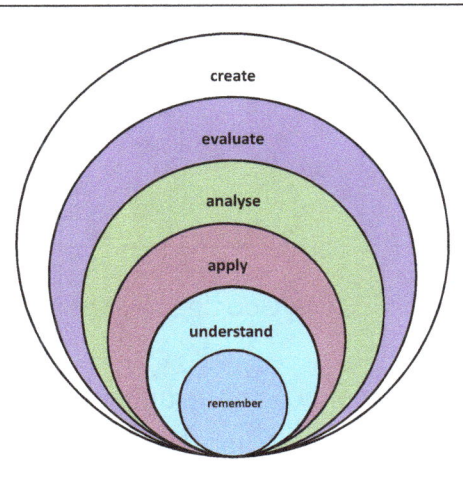 Bloom's Taxonomy Domains	1. Choose a concept you want to teach or develop and be clear of the attributes. e.g.: predatory animals, even numbers, living/non-living, etc. 2. Develop 'examples', 'non-examples', and 'test examples' for the concept – ensure these allow many different hypotheses. 3. Divide the class into small groups. 4. Present to the class the list of YES attributes in the form of images or words. 5. Ask students to discuss in their groups and guess what the concept is. 6. Present to the class the list of NO attributes in the form of images or words. 7. Students now compare both sets to guess the concept. e.g.: | YES Examples | NO Examples | |---|---| | Pictures of: Crocodile Bird Lion Snake Human | Pictures of: Kangaroo Apple Tree Baby | 8. Accept and scribe all answers on the board. 9. Do not reveal the concept or provide clues and keep on presenting as many examples as possible until they get closer to the concept you have in mind. 10. Provide each group with the 'test examples' and ask students to separate into YES and NO categories (10 minutes). 11. Walk around the class and facilitate students through leading questions. 12. Reveal the concept.

The Collaborative Classroom

CONCEPT ATTAINMENT

Cooperative Learning Elements	Additional Information
Face-to-Face/Promotive Interaction Safety and Individual Accountability Interpersonal/Social Skills Positive Interdependence ➢ Goal Interdependence ➢ Resource Interdependence ➢ Outside Force Interdependence ➢ Environmental Interdependence ➢ Simulation Interdependence	**When to use** • Use as a hook to grab students' attention and put them in a receptive frame of mind. • Before a new topic – check and activate prior knowledge. • Develop students' knowledge of concepts or new learning. • Reviewing a unit either at the beginning of a new lesson or at the end of a lesson. • Before an individual assignment – writing a type of text based on a genre. • Practising new skills - supporting students to apply new skills or concepts in different contexts. **TIPS** • Predetermine the outcome of this activity; (Review lesson/reflection of the lesson, report writing, public speaking, etc). • Simply turn chairs around if space is limited. • Pre-set home group stations for the rest of term/semester
Social Skills (to be pre-taught)	**Gradual Release Model**
Turn-taking Inside voices Active listening Respecting personal space Moving safely in the classroom How to disagree How to reach a consensus	<table><tr><th>I do</th><th>We do</th><th>You do</th></tr><tr><td></td><td>√</td><td>√</td></tr></table>
Online Ideas	• Tables in Google Docs/Google Sheets are effective options. • This strategy can only be done online. • Teachers may be able to use the breakout room feature via various online teaching platforms, if they have a small class.

DIALOGUE MAP

Instructional Strategy	Procedure
Dialogue Map **Bloom's Taxonomy Domains**	1. Divide class into small groups of 3-4 students. 2. Students have different roles – **WRITER, EDITOR, EVALUATOR, PRESENTER**. 3. Give each group an A3 paper with a topic or question: e.g.: Climate Change; 'How can we beat Covid-19?' 4. Students write individual ideas below the topic or question (3-5 minutes). 5. Students discuss and expand all the ideas by adding 'pro' and 'con' arguments and highlighting them using different colours (10 minutes). 6. The **EVALUATOR** picks one of the ideas and the **WRITER** writes a summary using all the notes (10 minutes). 7. The **EDITOR** edits the summary before the **PRESENTER** presents this to the whole class. 8. Teacher gives feedback on their summary. 9. Students repeat Steps 6 and 7 and complete a summary on another one of their ideas.

The Collaborative Classroom

DIALOGUE MAP

Cooperative Learning Elements	Additional Information
Face-to-Face/Promotive Interaction Safety and Individual Accountability Interpersonal/Social Skills Positive Interdependence: ➤ Goal Interdependence ➤ Resource Interdependence ➤ Outside Force Interdependence ➤ Environmental Interdependence	**When to use** • Use as a hook to grab students' attention and put them in a receptive frame of mind. • Before a new topic – check and activate prior knowledge. • Develop students' knowledge of concepts or new learning. • Reviewing a unit either at the beginning of a new lesson or at the end of a lesson. • Before an individual assignment – writing a type of text based on a genre. • Practising new skills - supporting students to apply new skills or concepts in different contexts. **TIPS** • Predetermine the outcome of this activity: (Summary writing, report writing, public speaking, etc). • Simply turn chairs around if space is limited. • Use both inside and outside classroom areas if required. • Teachers can assign the same question to all the groups OR each group could have a different question based on the same topic they are learning.
Social Skills (to be pre-taught)	**Gradual Release Model**
Turn-taking Inside voices Active listening Respecting personal space Moving safely in the classroom How to disagree How to reach a consensus	<table><tr><th>I do</th><th>We do</th><th>You do</th></tr><tr><td></td><td></td><td>√</td></tr></table>
Online Ideas	• Assign groups and students can use a table on google docs to write their ideas. • They can then present their ideas on various online learning platforms.

©Boney Nathan & Seetal Kaur 2021

FISHBOWL

Instructional Strategy	Procedure
Fishbowl Bloom's Taxonomy Domains (create, evaluate, analyse, apply, understand, remember)	1. This is an effective big group discussion tool. 2. Students sit in an outside and inside circle – see image. 3. The inside circle (the fishbowl) will discuss the topic that has been pre-determined by the teacher, or any current topic picked by students. 4. The teacher pre-determines time for the discussion. 5. The teacher can be in the first inside group to model the process. 6. Alternately, the teacher can provide an outline script to help keep the discussion going. 7. The outside circle students listen, take notes, and reflect. 8. Then four students from the outside circle switch places and do the same. They can use their reflections to agree/disagree with earlier discussion points. 9. This can go on until all students have had a chance to contribute to the discussion. 10. Teacher can collate all the points using the board or a word document. 11. Students then use these points to complete individual work that has been pre-determined by the teacher prior to this activity.

FISHBOWL

Cooperative Learning Elements	Additional Information
Face-to-Face/Promotive Interaction Safety and Individual Accountability Interpersonal/Social Skills Positive Interdependence ➤ Outside Force Interdependence ➤ Environmental Interdependence	**When to use** • Before a new topic – check and activate prior knowledge. • Develop students' knowledge of concepts or new learning. • Reviewing a unit either at the beginning of a new lesson or at the end of a lesson. • Before an individual assignment – writing a type of text based on a genre. • Practising new skills - supporting students to apply new skills or concepts in different contexts. **TIPS** • Use both inside and outside classroom areas if required. • If the class is very large, divide into groups of 10-15 and make the appropriate number of circles.
Social Skills (to be pre-taught)	**Gradual Release Model**
Turn-taking Inside voices Active listening Moving safely in the classroom How to disagree	<table><tr><th>I do</th><th>We do</th><th>You do</th></tr><tr><td>√</td><td>√</td><td>√</td></tr></table>
Online Ideas	• Can be done by pre-selecting the inside and outside students and switching after time is up. • Can be done using breakout rooms and teacher can float in and out of these rooms to facilitate discussions.

FISHBONE

Instructional Strategy	Procedure
Fishbone *[Fishbone diagram image showing cause-and-effect structure with branches labeled METHODS, MACHINERY, MANAGEMENT, MATERIALS, MANPOWER leading to EFFECT]* *[Bloom's Taxonomy nested circles diagram showing from inner to outer: remember, understand, apply, analyse, evaluate, create]* **Bloom's Taxonomy Domains**	1. This is an effective "cause and effect" mind mapping tool. 2. Write question or statement that is being investigated in the centre of the 'head'. 3. Decide how many causes that you want your students to explore. 4. Divide your students into groups – numbers in each group will depend on how many causes you have pre-determined. 5. Provide each group with an A3 paper. 6. Model the process using a different question/statement. Show students how they can draw the fishbone (refer to the image on the left). 7. Each main bone coming out of the middle will be the cause. The smaller lines from the main bones will explore the causes further. 8. Students work in their groups and each student will explore and write one main cause and three explorations of the cause. 9. Allow enough time to do this depending on the competency of your students. 10. They can discuss as they work. 11. At the end of the time given, students are given a further 5-10 minutes to collate all their ideas. 12. Students present their findings to the whole class. 13. They can then work individually or in pairs to produce the end product – pre-determined by the teacher.

FISHBONE

Cooperative Learning Elements	Additional Information
Face-to-Face/Promotive Interaction Safety and Individual Accountability Interpersonal/Social Skills Positive Interdependence ➢ Goal Interdependence ➢ Resource Interdependence ➢ Outside Force Interdependence ➢ Environmental Interdependence	**When to use** • Before a new topic – check and activate prior knowledge. • Develop students' knowledge of concepts or new learning. • Reviewing a unit either at the beginning of a new lesson or at the end of a lesson. • Before an individual assignment – writing a type of text based on a genre – very effective for persuasive texts. • Practising new skills - supporting students to apply new skills or concepts in different contexts – debates, speech, etc. **TIPS** • Predetermine the outcome of this activity: (Review lesson/reflection of the lesson, report writing, public speaking, etc). • Simply turn chairs around if space is limited. • Use both inside and outside classroom areas if required. • Pre-set groups before the lesson to minimise movement. • Control movement by releasing one group at a time.
Social Skills (to be pre-taught)	**Gradual Release Model**
Turn-taking Inside voices Active listening Respecting personal space Moving safely in the classroom How to disagree How to reach a consensus	<table><tr><th>I do</th><th>We do</th><th>You do</th></tr><tr><td>√</td><td>√</td><td>√</td></tr></table>
Online Ideas	• Tables in Google Docs/Google Sheets are effective options. • Students may be able to collaborate and present their findings via various online learning platforms.

©Boney Nathan & Seetal Kaur 2021

FIX IT

Instructional Strategy	Procedure
Fix it	1. Put students in groups of 4-6. 2. Have a demonstration round if your class is doing this activity for the first time. 3. Provide each group with a set of statements that consist of incorrect structure. e.g.: for Literacy: A) My uncle are a doctor. B) Yesterday, my mother will be cooking chicken rice. C) For you to be successful, you have to maintaining a high levels of patience. D) I don't mind having either tea nor coffee. 4. Students find the incorrect answers for the statements given (about 5-10 minutes – time factor depends on the number of statements given as well as the level of difficulty). 5. Once all the incorrect features have been identified, students fix the statements. (about 5-10 minutes) 6. Once the time is up, get each group to share and justify one of their answers. 7. The other groups will check their responses.
Bloom's Taxonomy Domains (create, evaluate, analyse, apply, understand, remember)	

©Boney Nathan & Seetal Kaur 2021

FIX IT

Cooperative Learning Elements	Additional Information

Face-to-Face/Promotive Interaction
Safety and Individual Accountability
Interpersonal/Social Skills
Positive Interdependence
    ➤ Goal Interdependence
    ➤ Resource Interdependence
    ➤ Outside Force Interdependence
    ➤ Environmental Interdependence
	When to use<ul><li>Use as a hook to grab students' attention and put them in a receptive frame of mind.</li><li>Before a new topic – check and activate prior knowledge.</li><li>Develop students' knowledge of concepts or new learning.</li><li>Reviewing a unit either at the beginning of a new lesson or at the end of a lesson.</li><li>Before an individual assignment – writing a type of text based on a genre.</li><li>Practising new skills - supporting students to apply new skills or concepts in different contexts.</li></ul>**TIPS**<ul><li>Predetermine the purpose of this activity; (Review lesson/reflection of the lesson, report writing, public speaking, etc).</li><li>Simply turn chairs around if space is limited.</li><li>This activity can be used in other subject areas such as Numeracy, Science, etc.</li></ul>

Social Skills (to be pre-taught)	**Gradual Release Model**
Turn-taking Inside voices Active listening Respecting personal space Moving safely in the classroom How to disagree How to reach a consensus	<table><tr><th>I do</th><th>We do</th><th>You do</th></tr><tr><td>√</td><td>√</td><td>√</td></tr></table>
Online Ideas	<ul><li>Tables in Google Docs/Google Sheets are effective options.</li><li>Students may be able to collaborate and present their findings via various online learning platforms.</li></ul>

FOUR CORNERS

Instructional Strategy	Procedure
Four Corners STRONGLY AGREE · AGREE STRONGLY DISAGREE · DISAGREE Bloom's Taxonomy Domains (create, evaluate, analyse, apply, understand, remember)	1. Generate a list of statements related to your topic of study. 2. Put up four labels (STRONGLY AGREE, AGREE, DISAGREE, STRONGLY DISAGREE) on different corners of the room. 3. Read the first statement to the class, e.g.: "Mobile phones should be banned at schools". 4. Allow time for students to independently think about a response to the statement. 5. Students' responses should be in the form of the four opinions; STRONGLY AGREE, AGREE, DISAGREE, STRONGLY DISAGREE. 6. They write down their reasons in their exercise books to justify their responses (about 3-5 minutes). 7. Once the time is up, students gather at the corner that corresponds to their responses. 8. They share their justifications (about 5-10 minutes). Time will vary depending on the number of students at each corner. 9. Inform students that a representative will be asked to share a summary of the discussion. 10. Once the time is up, call on a representative from each corner to present a group summary of their opinions. 11. When all summaries have been presented, students can change their opinions and move to their new corner. 12. Steps 5-13 are repeated with different statements.

©Boney Nathan & Seetal Kaur 2021

FOUR CORNERS

Cooperative Learning Elements	Additional Information
Face-to-Face/Promotive Interaction Safety and Individual Accountability Interpersonal/Social Skills Positive Interdependence ➢ Goal Interdependence ➢ Role Interdependence ➢ Resource Interdependence ➢ Outside Force Interdependence ➢ Environmental Interdependence	**When to use** - Use as a hook to grab students' attention and put them in a receptive frame of mind. - Before a new topic – check and activate prior knowledge. - Develop students' knowledge of concepts or new learning. - Reviewing a unit either at the beginning of a new lesson or at the end of a lesson. - Before an individual assignment – writing a type of text based on a genre. - Practising new skills - supporting students to apply new skills or concepts in different contexts. **TIPS** - Predetermine the outcome of this activity; (Review lesson/reflection of the lesson, report writing, public speaking, etc). - Have a demonstration round if your class is playing for the first time. - Use both inside and outside classroom areas if required.
Social Skills (to be pre-taught)	**Gradual Release Model**
Turn-taking Inside voices Active listening Respecting personal space Moving safely in the classroom How to disagree How to reach a consensus	<table><tr><th>I do</th><th>We do</th><th>You do</th></tr><tr><td>√</td><td>√</td><td>√</td></tr></table>
Online Ideas	- Tables with the four opinion headings in Google Docs/Google Sheets are effective options. - Teachers may be able to use the breakout room feature via various online teaching platforms.

©Boney Nathan & Seetal Kaur 2021

FRAYER MODEL

Instructional Strategy	Procedure

Frayer Model
 	
Definition: / Characteristics: / WORD: / Examples: / Non-examples:
 	
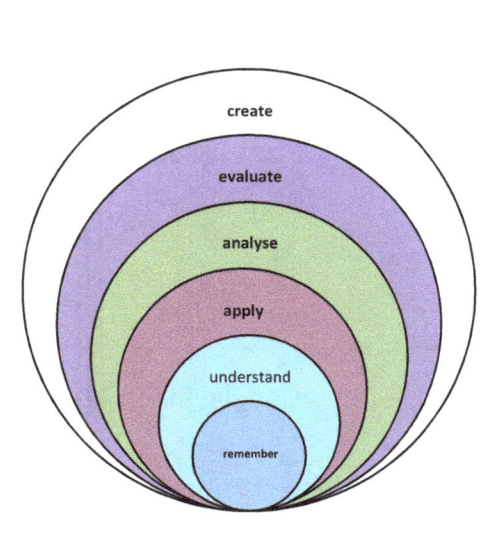
Bloom's Taxonomy Domains
	1. Students work in pairs or small groups.
	2. Introduce the graphic organiser; Frayer Model to students - Explain the four sections of the model and the big circle in the centre.
	3. Once students are familiar with the model, get them to write the vocabulary that is being introduced in the centre. e.g.: 'Mammals'
	4. Point to the upper left-hand corner and read the heading - Definition.
	5. Explain to students that they will write the definition of the word in that section (about 2-5 minutes, depending on the level of the students).
	    e.g.: Mammals are warm-blooded animals that give birth to babies, have fur, and breastfeed their babies.
	6. Move to the upper right-hand corner and read the heading - Characteristics.
	7. Explain to students that in this corner, they will list the characteristics or qualities of the word in the middle (about 2-5 minutes).
	    e.g.: warm-blooded, have hair or fur, give birth, feed milk to their babies, etc.
	8. Once that is completed, move to the Examples section.
	9. Explain to students that they are to list examples or provide synonyms of the word (about 2-5 minutes).
	    e.g.: Dogs, cats, tigers, etc.
	10. Point to the lower right-hand corner and read the heading - non-examples.
	11. Explain to students that they will list non-examples or provide antonyms of the vocabulary (about 2-5 minutes).
	    e.g.: Crocodiles, chickens, birds, ducks, etc.
	12. Once the time is up, get students to share their work with the rest of the class.
	13. Students can take notes while other students are presenting their findings.
	14. Repeat Steps 4-13 by introducing more new words/vocabulary to students.

FRAYER MODEL

Cooperative Learning Elements	Additional Information
Face-to-Face/Promotive Interaction Safety and Individual Accountability Interpersonal/Social Skills Positive Interdependence ➢ Goal Interdependence ➢ Resource Interdependence ➢ Outside Force Interdependence ➢ Environmental Interdependence	**When to use** • Use as a hook to grab students' attention and put them in a receptive frame of mind. • Before a new topic – check and activate prior knowledge. • Develop students' knowledge of concepts or new learning. • Reviewing a unit either at the beginning of a new lesson or at the end of a lesson. • Before an individual assignment – writing a type of text based on a genre. • Practising new skills - supporting students to apply new skills or concepts in different contexts. **TIPS** • Predetermine the outcome of this activity; (Review lesson/reflection of the lesson, report writing, public speaking, etc). • Simply turn chairs around if space is limited. • Allow extra time for advanced students to complete this activity individually.
Social Skills (to be pre-taught)	**Gradual Release Model**
Turn-taking Inside voices Active listening Respecting personal space Moving safely in the classroom How to disagree How to reach a consensus	<table><tr><th>I do</th><th>We do</th><th>You do</th></tr><tr><td>√</td><td>√</td><td>√</td></tr></table>
Online Ideas	• Tables in Google Docs/Google Sheets are effective options. • Students may be able to collaborate and present their findings via various online learning platforms.

GRAFFITI WALL

Instructional Strategy	Procedure

Graffiti Wall *Bloom's Taxonomy Domains*	1. Put up sheets of paper with different topics/questions around the classroom - same as the number of groups you have.
	2. Put students in groups of 3- 4 (depending on the size of the class or the topics/questions).
	3. Each student in the group is given a role: **Writer**, **Reader**, **Evaluator**, and **Manager/Timekeeper**.
	4. Station each group at their respective starting sheets.
	5. Each group is given a different coloured marker to write down their responses.
	6. Students will respond to the questions on the sheets (10 minutes).
	7. Once the time is up, signal each group to move to the next sheet.
	8. At the new station, students (10 minutes):
	   i. read the question,
	   ii. read and respond to the answer(s) written by the previous group(s) - '**√√**' if agree, '**√**' if unsure and '**?**' if they want more information,
	   iii. add their own ideas.
	9. The process is repeated until the groups arrive back at their starting point.
	10. The '**?**' in each sheet is directed to the group that wrote the statement or answer.
	11. Get the groups to read and share all the information on their sheets.

The Collaborative Classroom

GRAFFITI WALL

Cooperative Learning Elements	Additional Information
Face-to-Face/Promotive Interaction Safety and Individual Accountability Interpersonal/Social Skills Positive Interdependence ➢ Role Interdependence ➢ Resource Interdependence ➢ Outside Force Interdependence ➢ Environmental Interdependence	**When to use** • Use as a hook to grab students' attention and put them in a receptive frame of mind. • Before a new topic – check and activate prior knowledge. • Develop students' knowledge of concepts or new learning. • Reviewing a unit either at the beginning of a new lesson or at the end of a lesson. • Before an individual assignment – writing a type of text based on a genre. • Practising new skills - supporting students to apply new skills or concepts in different contexts. **TIPS** • Predetermine the outcome of this activity: (Review lesson/reflection of the lesson, report writing, public speaking, etc). • Use both inside and outside classroom areas if required.
Social Skills (to be pre-taught)	**Gradual Release Model**
Turn-taking Inside voices Active listening Respecting personal space Moving safely in the classroom How to disagree How to reach a consensus	<table><tr><th>I do</th><th>We do</th><th>You do</th></tr><tr><td></td><td></td><td>√</td></tr></table>
Online Ideas	• Tables in Google Docs/Google Sheets are effective options.

LITERATURE CIRCLES

Instructional Strategy	Procedure
Literature Circles	1. Group students into homogenous reading groups (5-6 students per group). 2. Each group decides on a book that they want to read and negotiate this with the teacher. 3. When you have agreed on the book, have a discussion with the group and explicitly explain what they will be doing (refer to notes on pages 75-76). 4. Give a copy of the notes to each group. 5. Set aside time for the process to take place (4-5 lessons). 6. Allow students to conduct their literature circles during these lessons. 7. Facilitate discussions – rotate through by facilitating one group per lesson.
Bloom's Taxonomy Domains (create, evaluate, analyse, apply, understand, remember)	

The Collaborative Classroom

LITERATURE CIRCLES

Cooperative Learning Elements	Additional Information

Face-to-Face/Promotive Interaction
Safety and Individual Accountability
Interpersonal/Social Skills
Positive Interdependence
  ➤ Goal Interdependence
  ➤ Role Interdependence
  ➤ Resource Interdependence
  ➤ Outside Force Interdependence
  ➤ Environmental Interdependence
	When to use
	• Develop students' knowledge of concepts or new learning.
	• Before an individual assignment – writing a type of text based on a genre.
	• Practising new skills - supporting students to apply new skills or concepts in different contexts.
	
	TIPS
	• Predetermine the outcome of this activity: (Review lesson/reflection of the lesson, report writing, public speaking, etc.).
	• Simply turn chairs around if space is limited.
	• Use both inside and outside classroom areas if required.

Social Skills (to be pre-taught)	**Gradual Release Model**
Turn-taking Inside voices Active listening Respecting personal space Moving safely in the classroom How to disagree How to reach a consensus	<table><tr><th>I do</th><th>We do</th><th>You do</th></tr><tr><td></td><td>√</td><td>√</td></tr></table>
Online Ideas	• Tables in Google Docs/Google Sheets are effective options. • Students may be able to collaborate and present their findings via various online learning platforms.

LITERATURE CIRCLE NOTES

What is a Literature Circle?	Your responsibility:
• You will work in small groups. • Your group will choose a book and everyone in the group will read the same book. • You will each have a role to help with your discussions. • You will rotate the roles so everyone gets a chance to do different things during each discussion. • We will continue our discussions over a few lessons.	• Read the agreed chapter/page each week. • Prepare your notes – this depends on your role for the week. • Share your thoughts/notes with your group during the Literature Circle time.

Your roles and what they mean:

Role Name	What you need to do	Some suggestions/Ideas
Discussion Director	You need to: ➢ write down a list of questions about the part you are reading today. ➢ help your group members talk about the big ideas and share their reactions ➢ direct the discussion by asking each group member what they were supposed to do and what they have completed ➢ work with your group to complete the daily report at the end of the discussion	• Who is the audience for this book? • How do you feel about……? • Was there anything that disturbed you? Why? • Was there anything difficult to read? Why? • What would adults say about ……? • What do you think will happen next? • What did this part of the book make you think about?
Literary Luminary/ Star/ Passage Picker	You need to find 3 sections or parts of the chapter that your group would enjoy reading aloud.	e.g.: Page…paragraph… Pick something that is funny, confusing, surprising etc.
Illustrator/Artist	You need to: ➢ draw a picture that is connected to what your group is reading today. ➢ write a caption to describe your drawing. ➢ talk about your drawing and why you chose it.	e.g.: a picture, a labelled diagram, a mind map, a story map etc. "I noticed…"
Connector	You need to: ➢ make three types of connections: • **Text-to-self** – connection between what you read and your past experience. • **Text-to-text** – connection between what you read and	**Text-to-self** – did you have any similar experiences or feelings? **Text-to-text** – any similar settings, characters, storyline, genre, etc.?

LITERATURE CIRCLE NOTES

	something you have read before. • **Text-to-world** – connection between what you read and what is happening in your community or the world. ➢ make notes of these connections and share with your group. ➢ ask other group members to share any connections that they have made.	**Text-to-world** – anything similar happening in the community, society, world? "I made a connection..."
Vocabulary Master	You need to: ➢ note down any difficult or unfamiliar words. ➢ share your notes with your group.	e.g.: a word map <table><tr><td>My word</td><td></td></tr><tr><td>Meaning</td><td></td></tr><tr><td>Synonyms</td><td></td></tr><tr><td>Antonyms</td><td></td></tr><tr><td>Picture</td><td></td></tr><tr><td>Sentence</td><td></td></tr></table>
Summariser	You need to list down some important points from the part your group is reading.	e.g.: • The main point the writer is making……. • The most important idea is… • In my own words… • This is how I would explain this part to someone else…
Travel Tracker	You need to track and record what is happening in the book.	You could use a diagram, map, mind map, etc.
Investigator	You need to find some background information about the book.	• What is the author's background? • What is the history behind the book?

Some suggestions on how you can start your discussion	Some suggestions on how you can agree/disagree	Some suggestions on how you can have end of book discussion
I wondered… I appreciated… I felt… I learned… I was surprised by….	Excuse me . . . I'd like to add . . . I disagree . . . I agree because . . . I don't understand what you mean . . . I'm confused about . . . That's an interesting idea, but I think…	• How did you feel about this book? • Would you recommend it? Why? • Would you read other books by the same author? Why? • What was the message of this story? • Name your favourite character? Why? • What is another possible ending to this story?

LOOP IT

Instructional Strategy	Procedure

Loop It	1. This is an effective vocabulary / checking of concept activity.
	2. Give each student a card.
	3. Half the class will have questions and half the class will have answers.
	4. Check for understanding.
	5. Students walk around the room with their cards and one hand up in search of the matching card.
	e.g.: Math – Student A: 25 x 4 - 12 =?
	              Student B: 3x - 21 = 6. X =?
	              Student C: 9
	              Student D: 88
	Student A will need to find Student D, and Student B will need to find Student C.
	6. Students may approach anyone to try and match their cards.
	7. If the cards match, the pair moves to the corner of the room and waits for others to finish.
	8. If the cards do not match, students continue to raise their hands, move around the class to find another partner.
	9. Steps 4-7 continue until all cards have been matched or until the time is up.
	10. Review answers for accuracy.

Bloom's Taxonomy Domains	

LOOP IT

Cooperative Learning Elements	Additional Information

Face-to-Face/Promotive Interaction
Safety and Individual Accountability
Interpersonal/Social Skills
Positive Interdependence
   ➢ Goal Interdependence
   ➢ Resource Interdependence
   ➢ Outside Force Interdependence
   ➢ Environmental Interdependence
	When to use
	• Use as a hook to grab students' attention and put them in a receptive frame of mind.
	• Before a new topic – check and activate prior knowledge.
	• Develop students' knowledge of concepts or new learning.
	• Reviewing a unit either at the beginning of a new lesson or at the end of a lesson.
	• Before an individual assignment – writing a type of text based on a genre.
	• Practising new skills - supporting students to apply new skills or concepts in different contexts.
	TIPS
	• Predetermine the outcome of this activity; (Review lesson/reflection of the lesson, report writing, public speaking, etc).
	• Use both inside and outside classroom areas if required.
	• Have a demonstration round if your class is playing for the first time.
	• To make the activity more challenging, increase the number of words or add description so that it involves more than 2 students.
	• This activity can be used in other subject areas such as Numeracy, Science, etc.

Social Skills (to be pre-taught)	**Gradual Release Model**
Turn-taking Inside voices Active listening Respecting personal space Moving safely in the classroom How to disagree How to reach a consensus	<table><tr><th>I do</th><th>We do</th><th>You do</th></tr><tr><td>√</td><td>√</td><td>√</td></tr></table>
Online Ideas	• This activity is not viable for online learning.

The Collaborative Classroom

NUMBERED HEADS TOGETHER

Instructional Strategy	Procedure

Numbered Heads Together	1. Put students in groups of 4-6.
	2. Number each student in the group; 1, 2, 3, 4, 5, 6.
	3. Read the first question/problem:
	  e.g.: Solve the equation: 6 x 2(1+2) =?
	  e.g.: Who were the allies in World War II?
	  e.g.: Name all the continents.
	4. Group members will put their heads together to discuss the answer (about 1 minute).
	5. Every member in a group should know the agreed upon answer(s).
	6. Roll a dice.
	7. Read the number that appears on the dice, e.g.: '5'.
	8. All the students with that number stand.
	9. One of the standing students is called upon to give their group's answer.
	10. Standing students with different answers can be called upon to explain their group's thinking.
	11. Repeat Steps 3-10 with the next question.

Bloom's Taxonomy Domains	

The Collaborative Classroom   79

NUMBERED HEADS TOGETHER

Cooperative Learning Elements	Additional Information

Face-to-Face/Promotive Interaction
Safety and Individual Accountability
Interpersonal/Social Skills
Positive Interdependence
   ➢ Goal Interdependence
   ➢ Outside Force Interdependence
   ➢ Environmental Interdependence
	When to use
	• Use as a hook to grab students' attention and put them in a receptive frame of mind.
	• Before a new topic – check and activate prior knowledge.
	• Develop students' knowledge of concepts or new learning.
	• Reviewing a unit either at the beginning of a new lesson or at the end of a lesson.
	• Before an individual assignment – writing a type of text based on a genre.
	• Practising new skills - supporting students to apply new skills or concepts in different contexts.
	TIPS
	• Alternatively, teacher can ask all students with the called number to record their group's answers on the board.
	• For questions with multiple answers, allow each standing student to report just one of their answers.
	• Ensure that students are aware that everyone is expected to be ready to talk for the group.
	• Simply turn chairs around if space is limited.

Social Skills (to be pre-taught)	**Gradual Release Model**
Turn-taking Inside voices Active listening Respecting personal space Moving safely in the classroom How to disagree How to reach a consensus	<table><tr><th>I do</th><th>We do</th><th>You do</th></tr><tr><td></td><td></td><td>√</td></tr></table>
Online Ideas	• Teachers can upload the list of questions onto Google Docs. • Use the breakout room feature from various online teaching platforms when students are instructed to put their heads together. Give students time to complete all questions. • Teachers can use an online dice.

PMI

Instructional Strategy	Procedure
PMI	1. Divide the class into pairs or small groups. 2. Pose a question or revisit a topic that has already been covered. 3. Model the PMI activity with the whole class using a simple question. e.g.: Students should be allowed to wear what they want when they come to school. 4. Students use the PMI template to discuss and note what they perceive as: **PLUS (P)** **MINUS (M)** **INTERESTING (I)** 5. Set time according to the complexity of the topic and your student context. 6. Alternatively, you can replace the **INTERESTING (I)** column with a **QUESTIONS (Q)** column. 7. Students share their thoughts and ideas with the whole class.
P | M | I table	
Bloom's Taxonomy Domains (create, evaluate, analyse, apply, understand, remember)	

The Collaborative Classroom

PMI

Cooperative Learning Elements	Additional Information

Face-to-Face/Promotive Interaction
Safety and Individual Accountability
Interpersonal/Social Skills
Positive Interdependence
    ➢ Goal Interdependence
    ➢ Resource Interdependence
    ➢ Outside Force Interdependence
    ➢ Environmental Interdependence
	When to use
	• Use as a hook to grab students' attention and put them in a receptive frame of mind.
	• Before a new topic – check and activate prior knowledge.
	• Develop students' knowledge of concepts or new learning.
	• Reviewing a unit either at the beginning of a new lesson or at the end of a lesson.
	• Before an individual assignment – writing a type of text based on a genre.
	• Practising new skills - supporting students to apply new skills or concepts in different contexts.
	TIPS
	• Predetermine the outcome of this activity: (Review lesson/reflection of the lesson, report writing, public speaking, etc).
	• Simply turn chairs around if space is limited.

Social Skills (to be pre-taught)	**Gradual Release Model**
Turn-taking Inside voices Active listening Respecting personal space Moving safely in the classroom How to disagree How to reach a consensus	<table><tr><th>I do</th><th>We do</th><th>You do</th></tr><tr><td>√</td><td>√</td><td>√</td></tr></table>
Online Ideas	• Tables in Google Docs/Google Sheets are effective options. • Teachers may be able to use the breakout room feature from various online teaching platforms when students are instructed to work in pairs or small groups.

QUIZ, QUIZ, TRADE

Instructional Strategy	Procedure
Quiz, Quiz, Trade | Front - Question 1	Back - Answer 1
Front - Question 2	Back - Answer 2 | Bloom's Taxonomy Domains (create, evaluate, analyse, apply, understand, remember)	1. Divide the class into 2 groups – A and B. 2. Provide each student with a card – a question on one side and the answer on the other side. 3. Have a demonstration round if your class is playing for the first time. 4. Get students to line up – Group A facing Group B. 5. A holds up their question to B – A can see the answer while B is responding. 6. When B answers – A will praise if the answer is correct; support and encourage if incorrect. 7. Now roles will reverse, and B will ask their question - B can see the answer while A is responding. 8. Time the whole process – about 3-5 minutes for each pair. 9. When time is up, they thank each other, exchange their cards, and move one step to left or right as pre-determined by the teacher. 10. Steps 4-7 are repeated with a new partner and new cards. 11. Keep going until at least half the class has had a chance to ask and answer.

QUIZ, QUIZ, TRADE

Cooperative Learning Elements	Additional Information
Face-to-Face/Promotive Interaction Safety and Individual Accountability Interpersonal/Social Skills Positive Interdependence ➢ Resource Interdependence ➢ Outside Force Interdependence ➢ Environmental Interdependence	**When to use** • Use as a hook to grab students' attention and put them in a receptive frame of mind. • Before a new topic – check and activate prior knowledge. • Develop students' knowledge of concepts or new learning. • Reviewing a unit either at the beginning of a new lesson or at the end of a lesson. • Before an individual assignment – writing a type of text based on a genre. • Practising new skills - supporting students to apply new skills or concepts in different contexts. **TIPS** • Predetermine the outcome of this activity: (Review lesson/reflection of the lesson, report writing, public speaking, etc). • Use both inside and outside classroom areas if required. • Use the stand-up → hand up → pair up method - teachers can pre-determine how many peers each student needs to talk to.
Social Skills (to be pre-taught)	**Gradual Release Model**
Turn-taking Inside voices Active listening Respecting personal space Moving safely in the classroom	<table><tr><th>I do</th><th>We do</th><th>You do</th></tr><tr><td>√</td><td>√</td><td>√</td></tr></table>
Online Ideas	• This activity is not viable for online learning.

SEND A PROBLEM

Instructional Strategy	Procedure
Send a Problem	1. Put students in groups of 3-4. 2. Provide each group with a sheet of paper that contains a question. 3. Each student is given a role; **WRITER**, **READER**, **EVALUATOR**, and possible **TIMEKEEPER**. 4. Each group is given a different coloured marker. 5. Students will respond to the questions assigned to their group (about 5-10 minutes). 6. Once the time is up, signal each group to pass their sheet to another group (this can be clockwise or anticlockwise). 7. Instruct the groups to read the new question first, then respond to the answer(s) written by the previous group(s). 8. Students now add their own ideas onto the paper before passing it to another group (about 5-10 minutes). 9. The process is repeated until each group receives their own question sheet back. 10. Students evaluate the responses written on the paper by all the groups. 11. Each group selects the best solution/answer for their problems. 12. They share their question and conclusion with the class.
Bloom's Taxonomy Domains (create, evaluate, analyse, apply, understand, remember)	

SEND A PROBLEM

Cooperative Learning Elements	Additional Information
Face-to-Face/Promotive Interaction Safety and Individual Accountability Interpersonal/Social Skills Positive Interdependence ➢ Goal Interdependence ➢ Role Interdependence ➢ Resource Interdependence ➢ Outside Force Interdependence ➢ Environmental Interdependence	**When to use** • Use as a hook to grab students' attention and put them in a receptive frame of mind. • Before a new topic – check and activate prior knowledge. • Develop students' knowledge of concepts or new learning. • Reviewing a unit either at the beginning of a new lesson or at the end of a lesson. • Before an individual assignment – writing a type of text based on a genre. • Practising new skills - supporting students to apply new skills or concepts in different contexts. **TIPS** • Predetermine the outcome of this activity; (Review lesson/reflection of the lesson, report writing, public speaking, etc). • Simply turn chairs around if space is limited.
Social Skills (to be pre-taught)	**Gradual Release Model**
Turn-taking Inside voices Active listening Respecting personal space Moving safely in the classroom How to disagree How to reach a consensus	<table><tr><th>I do</th><th>We do</th><th>You do</th></tr><tr><td></td><td></td><td>√</td></tr></table>
Online Ideas	• Tables in Google Docs/Google Sheets are effective options for students to type their answers and add on ideas. • Teachers may be able to use the breakout room feature from various online teaching platforms when students are instructed to work in pairs or small groups. • Students may be able to collaborate and present their findings via various online learning platforms.

STICKY NOTE GRAPHS

Instructional Strategy	Procedure
Sticky Note Graphs Bloom's Taxonomy Domains (create, evaluate, analyse, apply, understand, remember)	1. Present students with a question related to the content you are teaching. 2. Ensure that the question can tease out multiple correct answers or opinions. e.g.: Is climate change a hoax? Why? 3. Provide students with 5-10 sticky notes (This depends on the number of answers you anticipate). 4. Give them time to write one answer or response on each sticky note. (5 minutes) 5. When time is up students place their sticky notes on a designated area in the classroom. 6. You can create lines or tables for the students to place their sticky notes. 7. In the designated area, students work together to group sticky notes with similar answers or ideas. 8. Discuss common responses and explore reasons for similarities. 9. Leave the sticky notes during additional lessons and discussions. 10. Students can change their minds when they have had a chance to learn more about the topic.

STICKY NOTE GRAPHS

Cooperative Learning Elements	Additional Information
Face-to-Face/Promotive Interaction Safety and Individual Accountability Interpersonal/Social Skills Positive Interdependence ➢ Goal Interdependence ➢ Resource Interdependence ➢ Outside Force Interdependence ➢ Environmental Interdependence	**When to use** - Use as a hook to grab students' attention and put them in a receptive frame of mind. - Before a new topic – check and activate prior knowledge. - Develop students' knowledge of concepts or new learning. - Reviewing a unit either at the beginning of a new lesson or at the end of a lesson. - Before an individual assignment – writing a type of text based on a genre. - Practising new skills - supporting students to apply new skills or concepts in different contexts. **TIPS** - Predetermine the outcome of this activity; (Review lesson/reflection of the lesson, report writing, public speaking, etc). - Control movement by releasing one group at a time. - For larger classes, create more designated areas.
Social Skills (to be pre-taught)	**Gradual Release Model**
Turn-taking Inside voices Active listening Respecting personal space Moving safely in the classroom How to disagree How to reach a consensus	<table><tr><th>I do</th><th>We do</th><th>You do</th></tr><tr><td></td><td>√</td><td>√</td></tr></table>
Online Ideas	- Tables in Google Docs/Google Sheets are effective options. - Students may be able to collaborate via various online learning platforms.

Y CHART

Instructional Strategy	Procedure

Y Chart	1. Divide students into groups of 3-4.
	2. Provide an idea, concept, situation, image, real object, etc.
	3. Students observe and explore using their senses (about 5-10 minutes).
	4. They are allowed to discuss their observation and arrive at a consensus.
	5. Using the Y chart, they describe what it:
	   • LOOKS like
	   • SOUNDS like
	   • FEELS like – sensory or emotional depending on what has been provided for them to observe
	6. This can be adapted into an X chart if students need to describe TASTE as well.
	7. Students are consciously observing, actively listening, and deeply exploring touch/feeling.
	8. Students come up with as many adjectives as possible.
	9. These are then used to write a detailed description of what they have been asked to explore.

Bloom's Taxonomy Domains	

Y CHART

Cooperative Learning Elements	Additional Information
Face-to-Face/Promotive Interaction Safety and Individual Accountability Interpersonal/Social Skills Positive Interdependence ➤ Goal Interdependence ➤ Resource Interdependence ➤ Outside Force Interdependence ➤ Environmental Interdependence ➤ Simulation Interdependence	**When to use** - Use as a hook to grab students' attention and put them in a receptive frame of mind. - Before a new topic – check and activate prior knowledge. - Develop students' knowledge of concepts or new learning. - Reviewing a unit either at the beginning of a new lesson or at the end of a lesson. - Before an individual assignment – writing a type of text based on a genre. - Practising new skills - supporting students to apply new skills or concepts in different contexts. **TIPS** - Simply turn chairs around if space is limited. - Allow extra time depending on the task, student cohort etc. - Use both inside and outside classroom areas if required. - Have a demonstration round if your class is doing this activity for the first time.
Social Skills (to be pre-taught)	**Gradual Release Model**
Turn-taking Inside voices Active listening Respecting personal space Moving safely in the classroom How to disagree How to reach a consensus	<table><tr><th>I do</th><th>We do</th><th>You do</th></tr><tr><td>√</td><td>√</td><td>√</td></tr></table>
Online Ideas	- Students can be asked to have a list of things ready prior to the lesson. - Students may be able to collaborate via various online learning platforms to annotate a Y chart.

AUTHOR'S GALLERY WALK

Instructional Strategy	Procedure
Author's Gallery Walk  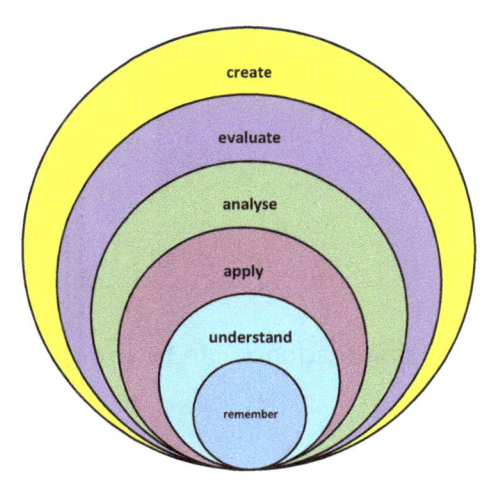 Bloom's Taxonomy Domains	1. This is a longer-term project. 2. Give students one or two weeks to complete the following tasks: 　➢ Write their own short story/poem/graphic novel etc. 　➢ Decide and organise how they will display it in the classroom – booklet, online, power point, etc. 　➢ They also need to organise a notebook or a digital forum for their classmates to leave comments about their work. 　➢ They can choose to use their own names or use a pseudonym 3. Set up areas around the classroom for students to display their work. 4. Allow students up to a week to read and leave comments for their classmates. 5. They can provide feedback individually, in pairs, or small groups. 6. Use a familiar text to model feedback strategies. 7. Explore important elements of effective writing to help students give their feedback. 8. Give students time to work in pairs to practise giving feedback using familiar texts. 9. Give samples on how to make comments on their friends' work. (refer to pages 93-94). 10. Comments can be done on sticky notes, notebooks, or digital forums. 11. Students then have feedback from all their classmates to help them improve on their writing.

The Collaborative Classroom

AUTHOR'S GALLERY WALK

Cooperative Learning Elements	Additional Information
Face-to-Face/Promotive Interaction Safety and Individual Accountability Interpersonal/Social Skills Positive Interdependence ➢ Goal Interdependence ➢ Outside Force Interdependence ➢ Environmental Interdependence	**When to use** • Develop students' knowledge of concepts or new learning. • Before an individual assignment – writing a type of text based on a genre. • Practising new skills - supporting students to apply new skills or concepts in different contexts. **TIPS** • You can also use this to solve Math problems, explore science concepts, etc. • Provide a roster for students to walk around and write their feedback.
Social Skills (to be pre-taught)	**Gradual Release Model**
Turn-taking Inside voices Active listening Respecting personal space Moving safely in the classroom How to disagree How to reach a consensus	<table><tr><th>I do</th><th>We do</th><th>You do</th></tr><tr><td>√</td><td>√</td><td>√</td></tr></table>
Online Ideas	• All work, including feedback can be in digital form.

AUTHOR'S GALLERY WALK COMMENT/FEEDBACK SAMPLE

Some ideas to give feedback:

Note: You can add as many ideas as you like. Make sure students have a copy to support them.

Something that you like	- I agree when you said _____ because _____ - One thing I learned was _____ - I enjoyed your writing because _____
Ask a question	- What do you mean by _____? - Where did you get your information? - Why did you write about _____?
Give one positive feedback	- Think about adding _____ - I'm confused about _____ - One thing that might make it better is _____

The Collaborative Classroom

AUTHOR'S GALLERY WALK COMMENT/FEEDBACK SAMPLE

Prompts	Suggested responses	Additional responses
Something that you like	<ul><li>I agree when you said _____ because _____</li><li>One thing I learned was _____</li><li>I enjoyed your writing because _____</li></ul>	
Ask a question	<ul><li>What do you mean by _____?</li><li>Where did you get your information?</li><li>Why did you write about _____?</li></ul>	
Give one positive feedback	<ul><li>Think about adding _____</li><li>I'm confused about _____</li><li>One thing that might make it better is _____</li></ul>	

BOOK TALK

Instructional Strategy	Procedure
Book Talk	1. Students are given time – around a week or two to pick a book of their choice and complete reading it. 2. They need to prepare a talk that will persuade their peers to read the book they are talking about. 3. They need to be ready to answer questions about their books. 4. Scaffold this through questionnaires, surveys, planning templates, etc. (refer to pages 97-98) 5. Model a talk using a book of your choice. 6. Have a clear set of rubrics on how their talks will be assessed. 7. Steps 4 to 6 are crucial as this is a highly accountable task. 8. Discuss the rubrics in class so students understand exactly what is expected of them. 9. Their talk time is pre-determined – usually not longer than five minutes and two minutes to answer questions. 10. Allow time for practice during lessons before the actual date – maybe ten minutes every day so they can practise with their peers. 11. Set aside enough time for students to complete their talks.
Bloom's Taxonomy Domains (create, evaluate, analyse, apply, understand, remember)	

BOOK TALK

Cooperative Learning Elements	Additional Information
Face-to-Face/Promotive Interaction Safety and Individual Accountability Interpersonal/Social Skills Positive Interdependence ➢ Goal Interdependence ➢ Outside Force Interdependence ➢ Environmental Interdependence	**When to use** • Develop students' knowledge of concepts or new learning. • Before an individual assignment – writing a type of text based on a genre. e.g.: A book review. • Practising new skills - supporting students to apply new skills or concepts in different contexts. **TIPS** • Predetermine the outcome of this activity; (Review lesson/reflection of the lesson, report writing, public speaking, etc). • Model the activity prior to student presentations.
Social Skills (to be pre-taught)	**Gradual Release Model**
Active Listening	<table><tr><th>I do</th><th>We do</th><th>You do</th></tr><tr><td>√</td><td></td><td>√</td></tr></table>
Online Ideas	• Students can present their talk through an online forum.

The Collaborative Classroom 96

BOOK TALK SCAFFOLDING

Steps to help you prepare your talk.

Purpose of the talk	To persuade your classmates to read the book you are talking about.
What do you need to include?	➢ Beginning - Something to catch the interest of your audience ➢ Middle - Information about your book ➢ End - Why is this book amazing?
Your steps	1. Pick a book that you loved or enjoyed reading. 2. Read it again. 3. Look at the questions below – see if you can answer as many as possible so you can include that in your talk. 4. Use your own words but you can have a few quotes from your book. 5. Think about ways on how you can keep your audience interested – what can make your talk different from someone else's? 6. Try to memorise your talk – you can have some reading cards with your main points on them. 7. Practise as much as you can – in front of the mirror, family members, friends etc.
On the day of your talk	➢ Bring your book with you. ➢ You will talk for five minutes. ➢ Your audience will be given two minutes to ask questions.

BOOK TALK SCAFFOLDING

Questions to help you prepare your talk.

Beginning	You could: 1. Ask an interesting question – for example, a fact or a place that you read about in the book. 2. You can ask the audience to close their eyes and imagine the setting you are describing. 3. You could read out an interesting conversation or description from your book. 4. You could role play the main character and say something weird or funny.
Middle	Choose a few questions from here to help you really describe the book you have chosen. Use quotes and examples from your book to help you do this. 1. What are the settings and themes of this book? 2. What conflicts and problems happened? 3. What are the important characteristics of the main characters? 4. Which part of the book did you enjoy the most and why? 5. What kept you going and not stop reading? 6. What effect did this book have on you? 7. What did you think it was going to be about – did that happen or were you surprised at what actually happened?
End	Choose a few questions from here to help you really describe the book you have chosen. Use quotes and examples from your book to help you do this. 1. Was this book easy or difficult to read? 2. Why do you think everyone should read this book? 3. What do you think they will remember for a long time? 4. What questions do you have about this book? 5. Why would you recommend this book?

CASE STUDIES

Instructional Strategy	Procedure
Case Studies	1. Divide class into small groups of three to four.
2. Give each group a different case or problem to investigate. Examples such as:
➢ How can we beat the covid-19 coronavirus?
➢ How can we educate people to stop consuming junk food?
➢ What do students want from school?
➢ How can we reduce our carbon footprint?
3. Pre-determine the end product – a report, a PowerPoint presentation, posters, etc.
4. Ensure students have been taught how to use analytical tools – graphs, surveys, interviews etc.
5. Give clear instructions and rubrics so students are well-informed of what is expected of them.
6. Rubrics can include questions such as:
➢ What is the problem?
➢ What is your goal?
➢ What are the facts?
➢ What do graphs, surveys, interviews, etc. show you?
➢ What is the conclusion you have reached?
➢ What are the recommendations that you propose?
7. This is a project so do allow time for completion – anywhere between 1 week to whole term depending on what students are being asked to investigate.
Bloom's Taxonomy Domains (create, evaluate, analyse, apply, understand, remember)	

CASE STUDIES

Cooperative Learning Elements	Additional Information
Face-to-Face/Promotive Interaction Safety and Individual Accountability Interpersonal/Social Skills Positive Interdependence ➢ Goal Interdependence ➢ Resource Interdependence ➢ Outside Force Interdependence ➢ Environmental Interdependence	**When to use** • Develop students' knowledge of concepts or new learning. • Before an individual assignment – writing a type of text based on a genre. • Practising new skills - supporting students to apply new skills or concepts in different contexts – problem solving, analytical reports, etc. **TIPS** • Predetermine the outcome of this activity: (a report, a PowerPoint presentation, posters, etc.)
Social Skills (to be pre-taught)	**Gradual Release Model**
Turn-taking Active Listening How to disagree How to reach a consensus	<table><tr><th>I do</th><th>We do</th><th>You do</th></tr><tr><td>√</td><td>√</td><td>√</td></tr></table>
Online Ideas	• Students can use online or social media platforms to meet and complete their project. • Students may be able to collaborate and present their findings via various online learning platforms. • Teachers may be able to use the breakout room feature from various online teaching platforms when students are instructed to work in pairs or small groups.

CAUSAL MAPPING

Instructional Strategy	Procedure

Causal Mapping

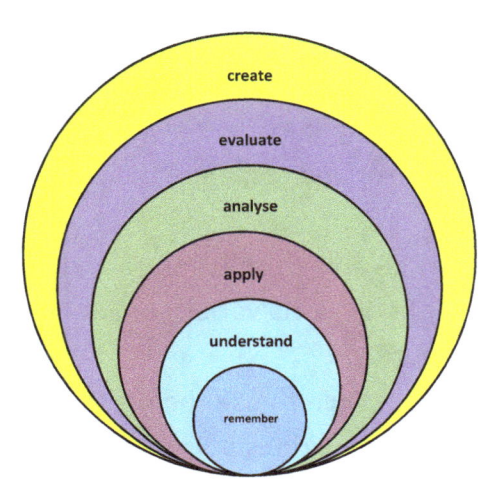
Bloom's Taxonomy Domains
	1. Divide class into small groups of 3-4.
	2. Give each group a different case or problem to investigate. Examples such as:
	    ➢ Covid-19
	    ➢ Obesity
	    ➢ Success at school
	    ➢ Carbon footprint
	3. Ensure students have been taught how to use analytical tools – graphs, surveys, interviews, etc.
	4. Model a mind-mapping tool to show how you use it to determine cause and effect – example Fishbone.
	5. Introduce 2-3 other mind mapping tools.
	6. Students must use one of these mind maps or any of their choice to show clear reasoning of cause and effect of their chosen topic.
	7. Give clear instructions and rubrics so students are well-informed of what is expected of them. Include mind mapping tools in the rubrics.
	8. Scaffolding can include questions such as:
	    ➢ What is the problem?
	    ➢ What are the causes? What are the effects?
	    ➢ What do graphs, surveys, interviews, etc. show you?
	    ➢ What is the conclusion you have reached?
	    ➢ What are the recommendations that you propose?
	9. This is a project so allow time for completion – anywhere between 1 week to the whole term depending on what students are being asked to investigate.

CAUSAL MAPPING

Cooperative Learning Elements	Additional Information
Face-to-Face/Promotive Interaction Safety and Individual Accountability Interpersonal/Social Skills Positive Interdependence ➢ Goal Interdependence ➢ Resource Interdependence ➢ Outside Force Interdependence ➢ Environmental Interdependence	**When to use** • Develop students' knowledge of concepts or new learning. • Before an individual assignment – writing a type of text based on a genre. • Practising new skills - supporting students to apply new skills or concepts in different contexts - problem solving, analytical reports, etc. **TIPS** • Predetermine the outcome of this activity: (a report, a PowerPoint presentation, posters, etc.)
Social Skills (to be pre-taught)	**Gradual Release Model**
Turn-taking Active Listening How to disagree How to reach a consensus	<table><tr><th>I do</th><th>We do</th><th>You do</th></tr><tr><td>√</td><td>√</td><td>√</td></tr></table>
Online Ideas	• Students can use online or social media platforms to meet and complete their project. • Students may be able to collaborate and present their findings via various online learning platforms. • Teachers may be able to use the breakout room feature from various online teaching platforms when students are instructed to work in pairs or small groups.

CUBING

Instructional Strategy	Procedure

Cubing
 	
Bloom's Taxonomy Domains (create, evaluate, analyse, apply, understand, remember)
	1. Group your students according to ability groups.
	2. Predetermine the outcome of this activity: (Report writing, public speaking, book review, etc).
	3. Prepare six questions based on what you want your students to explore.
	   e.g.: text analysis, vocabulary, concept, etc.
	4. You can use Bloom's taxonomy to guide your questions, so they increase in difficulty.
	5. You can either write or type out your questions on a cube template and make the cubes or you can use ordinary dice and have a set of numbered questions.
	6. Each group is given one cube template.
	7. Decide on the rules before students start playing:
	   ➢ Are students answering all 6 questions or are they stopping after they have answered 3 or 4 questions?
	   ➢ How many times can they pass?
	   ➢ Are they just answering the questions or writing down their answers in their books?
	8. Make sure your students are clear about the rules.
	9. Model the activity with a few students.
	10. Set aside time according to what you want to achieve.
	11. When allotted time is up, students should have enough information to complete individual work.

CUBING

Cooperative Learning Elements	Additional Information
Face-to-Face/Promotive Interaction Safety and Individual Accountability Interpersonal/Social Skills Positive Interdependence 　➢ Goal Interdependence 　➢ Resource Interdependence 　➢ Outside Force Interdependence 　➢ Environmental Interdependence	**When to use** • Use as a hook to grab students' attention and put them in a receptive frame of mind. • Before a new topic – check and activate prior knowledge. • Develop students' knowledge of concepts or new learning. • Reviewing a unit either at the beginning of a new lesson or at the end of a lesson. • Before an individual assignment – writing a type of text based on a genre. • Practising new skills - supporting students to apply new skills or concepts in different contexts. **TIPS** • Predetermine the outcome of this activity; (Review lesson/reflection of the lesson, report writing, public speaking, etc). • Simply turn chairs around if space is limited. • Use both inside and outside classroom areas if required. • Have a demonstration round if your class is playing for the first time.
Social Skills (to be pre-taught)	**Gradual Release Model**
Turn-taking Inside voices Active listening Respecting personal space Moving safely in the classroom How to disagree How to reach a consensus	<table><tr><td>I do</td><td>We do</td><td>You do</td></tr><tr><td>√</td><td>√</td><td>√</td></tr></table>
Online Ideas	• Teachers may be able to use the breakout room feature from various online teaching platforms. • Students can use online dice with the numbered questions. • Tables in Google Docs/Google Sheets are effective options.

INVENTORS

Instructional Strategy	Procedure
Inventors	1. Prepare a number of envelopes – same as the number of groups (3-4 students/group) you have.
2. Put a number of small objects in each envelope – blue tag, paper clip, a strand of wool, pop stick, rubber band etc.
3. Stick the instruction labels – (refer to labels on page 107) on the envelopes.
4. Hand out one envelope to each group.
5. Go through the instructions and check for understanding through questions.
6. Set time for students to begin and stop their inventions (5 minutes).
7. Students are allowed to discuss using home language or English as they work.
8. Students will present their inventions to the whole class when they are done.
Bloom's Taxonomy Domains	

INVENTORS

Cooperative Learning Elements	Additional Information

Face-to-Face/Promotive Interaction
Safety and Individual Accountability
Interpersonal/Social Skills
Positive Interdependence
    ➢ Goal Interdependence
    ➢ Resources Interdependence
    ➢ Outside Force Interdependence
    ➢ Environmental Interdependence
	When to use
	• Use as a hook to grab students' attention and put them in a receptive frame of mind.
	• Before a new topic – check and activate prior knowledge.
	• Develop students' knowledge of concepts or new learning.
	• Reviewing a unit either at the beginning of a new lesson or at the end of a lesson.
	• Before an individual assignment – writing a type of text based on a genre.
	• Practising new skills - supporting students to apply new skills or concepts in different contexts.
	
	TIPS
	• Use both inside and outside classroom areas if possible.
	• Simply turn chairs around if space is limited.

Social Skills (to be pre-taught)	**Gradual Release Model**
Turn-taking Inside voices Active listening Respecting personal space Moving safely in the classroom How to disagree How to reach a consensus	<table><tr><th>I do</th><th>We do</th><th>You do</th></tr><tr><td></td><td>√</td><td>√</td></tr></table>
Online Ideas	• This strategy can only be done online if students work individually. • Students can be asked to have a list of things ready prior to the lesson.

INVENTORS LABELS

INVENTORS

1. There are a few different items or things in the envelope.
2. Share them out in your group. Some students may have more than one.
3. Your group must use all the items.
4. You can only touch your own item.
5. Your group will invent or make a new product.
6. You have 5 minutes to complete your task.
7. When time is up, you will present or explain your product to the whole group.

INVENTORS

1. There are a few different items or things in the envelope.
2. Share them out in your group. Some students may have more than one.
3. Your group must use all the items.
4. You can only touch your own item.
5. Your group will invent or make a new product.
6. You have 5 minutes to complete your task.
7. When time is up, you will present or explain your product to the whole group.

INVENTORS

1. There are a few different items or things in the envelope.
2. Share them out in your group. Some students may have more than one.
3. Your group must use all the items.
4. You can only touch your own item.
5. Your group will invent or make a new product.
6. You have 5 minutes to complete your task.
7. When time is up, you will present or explain your product to the whole group.

INVENTORS

1. There are a few different items or things in the envelope.
2. Share them out in your group. Some students may have more than one.
3. Your group must use all the items.
4. You can only touch your own item.
5. Your group will invent or make a new product.
6. You have 5 minutes to complete your task.
7. When time is up, you will present or explain your product to the whole group.

INVENTORS LABELS

INVENTORS

1. There are a few different items or things in the envelope.
2. Share them out in your group. Some students may have more than one.
3. Your group must use all the items.
4. You can only touch your own item.
5. Your group will invent or make a new product.
6. You have 5 minutes to complete your task.
7. When time is up, you will present or explain your product to the whole group.

INVENTORS

1. There are a few different items or things in the envelope.
2. Share them out in your group. Some students may have more than one.
3. Your group must use all the items.
4. You can only touch your own item.
5. Your group will invent or make a new product.
6. You have 5 minutes to complete your task.
7. When time is up, you will present or explain your product to the whole group.

JIGSAW

Instructional Strategy	Procedure
Jigsaw	1. Divide class into small groups of 3-4 students using coloured paper or pop sticks. 2. Each group will have a member of each of the colours you are using. 3. This is the Home Group. 4. Display your topic of discussion or your question/s on the whiteboard. 5. Students will now break into groups of the same colour. 6. These will be called Expert Groups. 7. Give them a set time to discuss the topic or question (5-10 minutes depending on what is being asked). 8. Walk around and facilitate discussions to model/scaffold ideas. 9. After the set time is up, students return to their Home Groups. 10. They now have 3-4 "experts" who have brought back discussions and notes from their Expert Groups. 11. Each Home Group selects a: **Writer, Reader, Presenter,** and **Manager/Timekeeper**. 12. These roles can be pre-written on cards or the board, so they know exactly what they are meant to do. 13. Give them a set time to collate all their notes and prepare a presentation for the whole class (about 5-10 minutes). 14. They present their findings to the whole class. 15. Give them time to complete their individual writing based on all the research, note taking, and sharing they have completed.
Bloom's Taxonomy Domains	

JIGSAW

Cooperative Learning Elements	Additional Information

Face-to-Face/Promotive Interaction
Safety and Individual Accountability
Interpersonal/Social Skills
Positive Interdependence
   ➢ Goal Interdependence
   ➢ Resource Interdependence
   ➢ Outside Force Interdependence
   ➢ Environmental Interdependence
	When to use
	• Before a new topic – check and activate prior knowledge.
	• Develop students' knowledge of concepts or new learning.
	• Reviewing a unit either at the beginning of a new lesson or at the end of a lesson.
	• Before an individual assignment – writing a type of text based on a genre.
	• Practising new skills - supporting students to apply new skills or concepts in different contexts.
	TIPS
	• Pre-set home group stations and give out coloured cards or pop sticks as students enter the classroom.
	• Control movement by releasing one group at a time.
	• Use both inside and outside classroom areas if possible.
	• Simply turn chairs around if space is limited.

Social Skills (to be pre-taught)	**Gradual Release Model**
Turn-taking Inside voices Active listening Respecting personal space Moving safely in the classroom How to disagree How to reach a consensus	<table><tr><th>I do</th><th>We do</th><th>You do</th></tr><tr><td></td><td>√</td><td>√</td></tr></table>
Online Ideas	• Teachers may be able to use the breakout room feature via various online teaching platforms. • Tables in Google Docs/Google Sheets are effective options.

MIND MAPS

Instructional Strategy	Procedure
Mind Maps	1. Divide students into groups of 3-4.
2. Provide students with a question, concept, statement, etc. and an A3 sheet.
3. Model how a mind map works.
- Start in the centre – write the concept, question, etc. here
- Use many colours and pictures
- One keyword or phrase for every line that is starting from the centre to explore different aspects/ideas
- These then expand into 3 or 4 smaller thoughts or ideas
4. Provide enough time for deep exploration (about 20-30 minutes).
5. Encourage students to discuss and use reference materials to support opinions.
6. The maps can be used for various tasks – debates, genre-based writing, class presentations, etc.

Bloom's Taxonomy Domains

The Collaborative Classroom   111

MIND MAPS

Cooperative Learning Elements	Additional Information
Face-to-Face/Promotive Interaction Safety and Individual Accountability Interpersonal/Social Skills Positive Interdependence: ➢ Goal Interdependence ➢ Resource Interdependence ➢ Outside Force interdependence ➢ Environmental interdependence	**When to use** • Use as a hook to grab students' attention and put them in a receptive frame of mind. • Before a new topic – check and activate prior knowledge. • Develop students' knowledge of concepts or new learning. • Reviewing a unit either at the beginning of a new lesson or at the end of a lesson. • Before an individual assignment – writing a type of text based on a genre. • Practising new skills - supporting students to apply new skills or concepts in different contexts. **TIPS** • Predetermine the outcome of this activity: (Review lesson/reflection of the lesson, report writing, public speaking, etc). • Simply turn chairs around if space is limited. • Use both inside and outside classroom areas if required.
Social Skills (to be pre-taught)	**Gradual Release Model**
Turn Taking Inside Voices Active Listening Respecting Personal Space Moving Safely in the Classroom How to Disagree How to Reach Consensus	<table><tr><th>I do</th><th>We do</th><th>You do</th></tr><tr><td>√</td><td>√</td><td>√</td></tr></table>
Online Ideas	• Tables in Google Docs/Google Sheets are effective options for online discussions. • Students may be able to create their own mind maps and present their findings via various online learning platforms. • Students may use online mind map apps.

The Collaborative Classroom

THREE-ROLE INTERVIEW

Instructional Strategy	Procedure

Three-Role Interview
 	
Role 1: Interviewer, Interviewee, Note-taker
Role 2: Interviewee, Note-taker, Interviewer
Role 3: Note-taker, Interviewer, Interviewee
 	
Bloom's Taxonomy Domains (create, evaluate, analyse, apply, understand, remember)
	1. Predetermine the outcome of this activity: (Review lesson/reflection of the lesson, report writing, public speaking, etc).
	2. Pose a specific issue about the topic being discussed:
	e.g.: Effects of air pollution
	3. Check for understanding.
	4. Group students into groups of threes.
	Student A- **INTERVIEWER**
	→ asks probing questions.
	Student B- **INTERVIEWEE**
	→ answers questions from interviewer.
	Student C- **NOTE-TAKER**
	→ listens actively to the comments and thoughts of the interviewee, writes down key points and significant details.
	5. Allow about 5 minutes for this process to happen.
	6. Once the time is up, students switch roles:
	e.g.: Student A - **INTERVIEWEE**
	     Student B - **NOTE-TAKER**
	     Student C - **INTERVIEWER**
	7. The process is completed when all 3 students have had a turn for all the roles (refer to the image on the left).
	8. Teacher can call out volunteers from the class to share their discussions.

The Collaborative Classroom

THREE-ROLE INTERVIEW

Cooperative Learning Elements	Additional Information
Face-to-Face/Promotive Interaction Safety and Individual Accountability Interpersonal/Social Skills Positive Interdependence ➤ Goal Interdependence ➤ Role Interdependence ➤ Outside Force Interdependence ➤ Environmental Interdependence	**When to use** • Before a new topic – check and activate prior knowledge. • Develop students' knowledge of concepts or new learning. • Reviewing a unit either at the beginning of a new lesson or at the end of a lesson. • Before an individual assignment – writing a type of text based on a genre. • Practising new skills - supporting students to apply new skills or concepts in different contexts. **TIPS** • Adjust time according to student levels and context. • Simply turn chairs around if space is limited.
Social Skills (to be pre-taught)	**Gradual Release Model**
Turn-taking Inside voices Active listening Respecting personal space Moving safely in the classroom	<table><tr><th>I do</th><th>We do</th><th>You do</th></tr><tr><td></td><td></td><td>√</td></tr></table>
Online Ideas	• Teachers can upload the topic onto Google Docs. • Teachers may be able to use the breakout room feature from various online teaching platforms when students are instructed to work in pairs or small groups. • Students may be able to collaborate and present their findings via various online learning platforms.

WRITE 'N' PASS

Instructional Strategy	Procedure

Write 'n' Pass
 	
Bloom's Taxonomy Domains
	1. This is an effective activity for narrative writing.
	2. Provide each student with a piece of paper. Alternatively, students can use their books.
	3. Write the topic/question/title of the narrative on the board.
	   e.g.: My Unforgettable Experience
	4. Have a demonstration round if your class is doing this activity for the first time.
	5. Students are given 1 minute to write a sentence based on the title given.
	6. Once the time is up, each student passes their paper/book to the student next to them (this can be clockwise or anticlockwise).
	7. They read all the responses before adding their own idea/sentence.
	8. Spelling does not matter.
	9. Check for understanding.
	10. The process is repeated until their own pieces of paper/books return to them.
	11. Provide students with a checklist on what you want them to evaluate:
	   e.g.: Plot, Characterisation, Climax, etc.
	14. Each student reads and evaluates the ideas written by their classmates.
	15. This becomes a sample to guide their own writing.

WRITE 'N' PASS

Cooperative Learning Elements	Additional Information
Face-to-Face/Promotive Interaction Safety and Individual Accountability Interpersonal/Social Skills Positive Interdependence ➢ Goal Interdependence ➢ Resource Interdependence ➢ Outside Force Interdependence ➢ Environmental Interdependence	**When to use**<ul><li>Before a new topic – check and activate prior knowledge.</li><li>Develop students' knowledge of concepts or new learning.</li><li>Reviewing a unit either at the beginning of a new lesson or at the end of a lesson.</li><li>Before an individual assignment – writing a type of text based on a genre.</li><li>Practising new skills - supporting students to apply new skills or concepts in different contexts.</li></ul>**TIPS**<ul><li>Predetermine the purpose of this activity; (Review lesson/reflection of the lesson, report writing, public speaking, narrative writing, etc).</li><li>For larger classes, divide students into groups of 10-15 and make the appropriate number of circles.</li></ul>
Social Skills (to be pre-taught)	**Gradual Release Model**
Turn-taking Respecting personal space	<table><tr><th>I do</th><th>We do</th><th>You do</th></tr><tr><td>√</td><td>√</td><td>√</td></tr></table>
Online Ideas	<ul><li>Tables in Google Docs/Google Sheets are effective options.</li><li>Students add ideas to the designated rows/column on the tables.</li><li>Ensure that students have been divided into small groups of 5.</li></ul>

Inspired by the research of:

Johnson, D. W., Maruyama, G., Johnson, R., Nelson, D., & Skon, L. (1981). Effects of cooperative, competitive, and individualistic goal structures on achievement: A meta-analysis. *Psychological Bulletin*, 89(1), 47–62. https://doi.org/10.1037/0033-2909.89.1.47

Kagan, S. & Kagan, M. (2009). *Kagan Cooperative Learning*. San Clemente, CA: Kagan Publishing.

Lyman, F. (1981). The Responsive Classroom Discussion. In A. S. Anderson (Ed.), *Mainstreaming Digest* (pp. 109–113). College Park, MD: University of Maryland College of Education.